Books by the author:

The Courage to Encourage

Utmost(co-authored with Ashis Brahma MD)

Your Compassionate Nature

The Phoenix Miracle

How to overcome disasters,
losses and tragedies and soar to give
compassion, light and love to others

Elizabeth A. Garcia-Janis, MD

BALBOA.PRESS
A DIVISION OF HAY HOUSE

Balboa Press books may be ordered through booksellers or by contacting:

Balboa Press
A Division of Hay House
1663 Liberty Drive
Bloomington, IN 47403
www.balboapress.com
844-682-1282

Because of the dynamic nature of the Internet, any web addresses or
links contained in this book may have changed since publication and
may no longer be valid. The views expressed in this work are solely those
of the author and do not necessarily reflect the views of the publisher,
and the publisher hereby disclaims any responsibility for them.

The author of this book does not dispense medical advice or prescribe the use
of any technique as a form of treatment for physical, emotional, or medical
problems without the advice of a physician, either directly or indirectly. The
intent of the author is only to offer information of a general nature to help
you in your quest for emotional and spiritual well-being. In the event you use
any of the information in this book for yourself, which is your constitutional
right, the author and the publisher assume no responsibility for your actions.

Any people depicted in stock imagery provided by Getty Images are
models, and such images are being used for illustrative purposes only.
Certain stock imagery © Getty Images.

Print information available on the last page.

ISBN: 978-1-9822-5872-6 (sc)
ISBN: 978-1-9822-5873-3 (hc)
ISBN: 978-1-9822-5874-0 (e)

Library of Congress Control Number: 2020922840

Balboa Press rev. date: 11/17/2020

Dedication

This book is humbly dedicated to the
people I love and the people I serve.

My profound gratitude to all of you for
having taught me about the light that comes
from overcoming the challenges in life

Introduction

This book was compassionately born out of my firm belief that we can overcome disasters, losses and tragedies and thus allow us to soar beyond ourselves to give compassion and light to the world. Most of this book was written in parts over a period of more than a decade, driven not only by the thought that the challenges we face in our lives can make us stronger, but that our own healing can help others heal themselves.

Having experienced losses and tragedies, I learned that the light truly shines brightly within the darkness of our grieving spirits. Tragedies teach us that a higher force is in control. Disasters bring out the best in us when we choose to be of help and service to the down-trodden and those afflicted with its life-changing consequences.

It is my hope that this book can help people strengthen their resilience within and that most of all, to know that they are not alone. I have learned so much from the people who graced my personal and professional life. Their life stories have been incorporated in my being and helped me discern various ways to serve other people. After more than 40 years as a Child and Adult psychiatrist, I continue to understand that the most beautiful part of our souls is our sacred humanity.

Many of the concepts in this book have helped me cope with life in general. People have shared with me what helped them bounce back from their many difficult experiences. You will also notice that there are certain healing words used a lot in this book like "gentle", "love", "compassion". These common yet profound words serve as soft balms to what may be the emotional harshness of having gone through disasters, losses or tragedies.

The Gentle Reflective Questions in each sub-chapter, are the basic who, what, where, when, why questions that encourage us to try to go deeper into our selves to acquire insight that we need to overcome our problems.

The Phoenix Miracle Pearls are words of wisdom from some of my favorite thinkers of all times like Khalil Gibran, Jalaluddin Rumi, and William Shakespeare. Their words are laden with brilliance and serve to illuminate the path that can lead us to deal with some of life's trials and tribulations.

The Gentle Exercises for the Spirit can help us put into action the ideas that can walk us through our challenging times. They can serve to nourish our beings and hopefully help us cope more during painful circumstances in our lives.

Enough space was provided in the chapters of this workbook so the readers can write down some of their thoughts, insights and answers to the questions. The readers may also want to contemplate on the wise quotes and the exercises for the spirits.

The healing concepts in this book are quite simple, yet it is my hope that these could provide valuable insights on how we can utilize our inner strengths to heal and to eventually soar like the phoenix to give compassion and light to others. As our bodies can heal, so can our minds and our spirits.

May the "phoenix miracle" in all of us give light to ourselves and others.

With gratitude and love,
Elizabeth A. Garcia-Janis MD

Special Mention

The paintings of angels in this book were created by my beloved sister Marissa A. Garcia. She also brilliantly created the painting on the cover of this book. I was talking to her about the concept of a phoenix soaring towards the light and she manifested it in this beautiful and amazing painting.

This painting is also the icon for the non-profit organization I founded – The Phoenix Global Humanitarian Foundation. Marissa was a consummate artist and dedicated Expressive Therapist and is now painting with the angels in heaven.

She was my best friend.

Foreword

What challenges are we likely to face in our lifetimes?

We have no shortage of them, to be sure. Natural disasters, such as hurricanes, earthquakes and volcanic eruptions, as well as man-made ones, such as war and terrorism, exact a heavy toll on lives and property.

Early in 2020, the entire world began to realize the dire threat from the coronavirus pandemic that has already claimed many lives, leaving scientists scrambling to develop a vaccine that would cure the deadly infection.

And then there are those events and situations in daily life that sometimes turn out to be life-changing, or create deep-seated resentments, such as bullying, or becoming victim of criminal acts. But not all is doom and gloom from the disasters and tragedies that seem to befall us when we least expect them. Wasn't it the German philosopher Friedrich Nietzche who told us: "That which does not kill us, makes us stronger."

If that is so, how should we respond to the difficulties and problems that life throws our way? We can be overwhelmed by fear or hesitation and fall into the pit of self-doubt, depression and despair, and simply give up.

Or we can choose to confront them head-on with all the resources we can muster, and strive to surmount every hindrance that stands in our way. Taking the second course of action is how Psychiatry, the branch of medicine concerned with the diagnosis and treatment of mental disorders, and

Psychology, the scientific study of all forms of human behavior and the methods through which behavior can be modified, can help.

Dr. Elizabeth Garcia-Janis has been a psychiatrist in the US for the past 40 years. She is the author of three books dealing with her area of ex-pertise. In her fourth book, *The Phoenix Miracle*, she has written a self-help guide for dealing with various challenges people face as a result of disaster, loss and tragedy, and offers guidelines on how we can cope with various stresses in our daily lives.

The phoenix is a legendary Arabian bird said to set fire to itself and rise anew from the ashes every 500 years. Dr. Garcia-Janis uses this as a metaphor for self-healing and draws from her extensive training and experience in psychiatry to take readers on a journey of self-discovery and re-covery from anxiety to debilitating depression and other types of mental illness.

The Phoenix Miracle covers a wide range of topics grouped under three main headings: We Heal, We Rise, and We Soar.

Under We Heal, she lists down specific suggestions. Among these are to: Open our hearts and minds to our healing; Acknowledge our pain; Receive help and guidance with an open heart; and Surround ourselves with people who love us and who we love.

Under We Rise, there are more concrete suggestions: Rest, relax, take it easy; Meditate, cleanse our minds, un-clutter our hearts; Pray on our knees and walk in prayer; and, Be kind and gentle to ourselves.

And under We Soar, we have these: Embrace our faith even more; Practice compassion and kindness especially when it is hard to do; Learn to laugh at ourselves; Find perfection in people's imperfections, apologize; Open up to rainbows and delight in each color; Believe in our life purpose; and Volunteer, volunteer, volunteer.

As the reader will discover, this is a step-by-step guide to self-healing that opens up new ways of looking at ourselves, dealing with other people and interacting with our immediate environment.

I have known Dr. Elizabeth Garcia-Janis from our high school days at the University of the Philippines Preparatory School. A good number in our batch went on to study medicine and became specialists in their chosen fields.

Dr. Garcia-Janis chose to specialize in psychiatry to enable those whose lives have been turned upside down by tragedy and loss to see the light at the end of the tunnel. In so doing, she has assisted many people to find inner peace and experience rebirth.

This book will no doubt inspire many others to rise like the phoenix from the ashes of self-doubt, insecurity and helplessness. I'm sure many will find it a handy and convenient guide for us to make peace with our selves, and perhaps even make the world—our world—a better place to live in.

Ernesto "Butch" M. Hilario
Political Science
University of the Philippines

He has worked for government, non-profit/development, non-government organizations and the private sector as writer/editor/re-searcher.

Ernesto has also written articles on politics and culture for various newspapers and magazines, and now writes a weekly column for the Manila Standard broadsheet.

Strengthening The Path of Our Healing Journey

I. WE HEAL

II. WE RISE

III. WE SOAR

WE HEAL

1. Open our hearts and minds to our healing

Let us find our light, wherever we sense it to be - inside or outside of ourselves, or somewhere in between. The light could be everywhere or anywhere. Then let us hold on to that light with all our being, until we finally feel that we are able to let go.

That moment is when we know we can share our light with others.

But first, simply believe that we will heal and soar to be there for others. Believe that we are deeply and truly connected to those we love and to those who love us. If we find it difficult to believe that at first, we need not be too hard on ourselves. Our hesitation to believe is nothing more than old fears surfacing, a normal defensive reaction. It may arise from old wounds that are merely scars now. The scars remain in our awareness, but they do not hurt anymore. We can believe again.

It is through our belief that we can open our mind to the miracle within us that will allow us to soar to our highest self. That belief will lead us and empower us to heal others as we heal our selves.

I knew a woman named Eva, a vibrant, bright, lovable professional, loved well by most everyone who knew her. She was kind, compassionate, and always had a cheerful demeanor, but in her mid-thirties Eva received tragic news: an aggressive cancer had begun in her breast and spread to her lymph nodes. This was nothing less than a death sentence. Her family and friends were stricken with grief. Eva herself was dumbfounded, and more so lived in a state of numbness for a while, experiencing utter disbelief. Her husband of five years, who she loved dearly, was in horrible shock. She alternated between being withdrawn and depressed and being angry at what happened.

Then, at a moment when she felt like she just wanted to die, she heard her husband sobbing inconsolably in the next room. She walked into the doorway and witnessed his pain and his fear of losing her. It was her *"necessary jolt"* – the flash of insight that propelled her out of emotional paralysis. She suddenly felt that there was no more time needed to be wasted by going inside herself. She realized that she now needed to believe that what was happening to her could somehow help others.

Her husband was a good man who loved her dearly. She was not about to let him down by choosing emotional death. Eva decided to be an example to the many who suffer what she was suffering. At work, she became focused on championing a cause, a fundraising drive to create a new wing in a hospital that specialized in cancer treatment. This she did in between her chemotherapy appointments and recovery periods.

Many of her friends thought she might be in denial, and wondered about the consequences of her refusing to grieve. She told them that she had simply made a choice. She could go inward and thereby make what seemed to be the last moments of her life miserable for herself or others. Or she could open up her heart and mind to healing. And from that openness, she could choose to believe that she had it in her to live each day in her life with as much dignity and grace as possible.

Her family and relatives benefited from her positive attitude. Even during the harshness of her chemotherapy, her focus remained steady – to make sure that that hospital wing was built for those sick children in need. An illness was trying to ravage her body and emotions, yet she chose to hold the belief that each day was a gift. And since each day was a gift, she made sure that she treasured that gift and made full use of it by serving those whom she felt were more in need than her.

She went through remissions and exacerbations, but before finally passing away Eva spent three more years wholeheartedly devoted to her husband, her family, her work and her volunteerism. She did not give in. Nor did she give up on her life. Her deep desire was actualized, a desire to live out her best possible life in whatever amount of time would be granted her. There was a radiance about her, even when she felt terribly sick. When she was gone, it felt to those of us who loved her that she had simply gone to sleep. At the time of her diagnosis, her doctors believed she had only six months to live. Somehow, she lived four more years – most of them in a state of purposefulness and emotional strength. Her decision to open her mind and heart to heal was crucial.

Terrible pain, which visits every human life, often impels us to slam our emotional doors shut from the universe, and especially from the ones we love. But this Phoenix Miracle person realized that she could make a different kind of choice. Eva focused on the possibilities of healing and helping. She remained connected to humanity, and acted on her compassion for the pain her husband felt about losing her. Eva candidly told me that even though she knew it was possible that she could die even sooner than the predicted six months, she opened herself to all possibilities and intended to live her life fully and meaningfully. I will never stop feeling gratitude for the fruits of that decision, and for her living example of a Phoenix Miracle.

To honor our own very real potential to be just as magnificent in our lives, please spend time with the following:

Gentle Reflective Questions

1. When have you ever closed your mind and heart about something?
2. What stops you now, or at vulnerable moments, from opening your heart and mind to believe in your healing?
3. Who do you feel closest to? Who in your life helps you stay connected with life? (Write or think about as many people as you can)
4. What are the things that you enjoy doing? What makes life feel worthwhile?
5. If you were to open your mind and heart to your healing now, what do you think will happen?

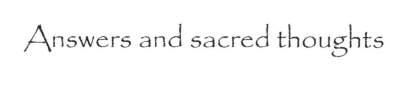

Answers and sacred thoughts

Phoenix Miracle Pearls

Here is a gentle thought to contemplate. As you nurture the possible meanings in your mind, may your time of reflection reveal Phoenix Miracle Pearls.

> "Tragedies and disasters are tillers of our souls. They help us evolve into more loving, more compassionate people."
>
> ~ author

> "Mostly it is loss that teaches us about the worth of things."
>
> ~ Unknown

Gentle Exercises of the Spirit

Let us spend a few minutes with these gentle thoughts. We may either repeat them to ourselves, or commit them to writing. Either way, they will gradually become rooted in our makeup, and help us become a Phoenix Miracle person:

"I will open my mind and heart to my healing."

"I will open my mind and heart to all possibilities."

With our eyes closed, let us visualize ourselves as we gently focus on these thoughts. Inhale slowly and softly, then exhale gently and slowly. Do this three times with each of the thoughts.

Then, softly whisper each thought to yourself. Say them slowly, gently, three times.

Allow ourselves to feel peace and serenity as we hear our own voice.

Next, move from gentle thoughts to gentle actions: With our eyes closed, let us open our arms very slowly, as wide as we can. Then bring our arms together as if hugging someone and ourselves snuggly and slowly. Then open our arms again, performing the action three times. As our arms move, we open ourselves to thoughts of what we might do in our mind and heart to serve someone else. Visualize ourselves opening our minds and hearts to something new. Then visualize ourselves opening our hearts and minds to experiencing a serene and peaceful self. Feel the deep comfort as we revisit these words: "I will open my heart and mind to my healing."

2. Acknowledge our pain.

Let us be honest with ourselves. Acknowledge ourselves. Let us look in the mirror. Stay kind and gentle as we look at ourselves. That image is us, looking at us. That image is you, looking at you. Practice honesty. Say our truth simply. Acknowledge that the loss, tragedy or disaster we have experienced has hurt us deeply. It has hurt us deeply because we love deeply.

After speaking our truth about our pain, let us temper our thoughts with compassion. The pain hurts. The truth hurts. Yet they are like booster shots, spiritual medicine that will help us heal ourselves, and in the future protect ourselves better from the vicissitudes of life.

Acknowledging our pain is one of the most important steps in our healing after any disaster, loss or tragedy occurs. Many times, these heartbreaking circumstances leave us numb and in a state of shock. This is because the mind has a way of initially protecting itself. But once it feels ready, it can allow us to be able to safely acknowledge, and intimately feel, the scope of our pain and loss.

My mother passed away, several years ago. At first I just felt numb. Then I went through so many mixed emotions about her death. She had been ill for a long time. I flew back to the Philippines just to bring back her ashes to my siblings and the rest of our extended family here in the USA. Many stressful logistics issues arose to make it even more difficult to fulfill this familial obligation. I had to suppress my emotions and feelings of grief in order to handle the situation. Once I came back home, those delayed emotions hit me hard. Grief can be gripping.

Once my tears slowed down a bit, I wrote a eulogy for my mother. It felt healing to be able to write and then verbalize how I felt. I acknowledged the pain. Self-honesty is quite a freedom-giver. It frees us from the shackles of inner pain. Many times, though, self-honesty can also be heart wrenching. Compassion must always be remembered, and mindfully included, so our honesty does not veer into emotional self-laceration or laceration of others. Compassion tempers our feelings to evoke a soulful sense of honesty from intolerable suffering. Though some would say that pain is inevitable and suffering is optional.

I wrote my eulogy for my mom from my heart. Without editing. I was able to express it simply. I looked in the mirror. I am my mother's daughter. And there was a reason and a purpose for her giving birth to me. Then, I contemplated upon a photograph of my mother, one taken when she was in her late teens. She looked so lovely. Her smile seemed shy and her eyes appeared soft. How young she was then, with her long, flowing dark brown to black hair. No wonder my dad was smitten by her. She looked so beautiful and innocent in that photo in its gilded oval frame. My cheekbones and eyes reminded me of hers. Every time I come home, when I walk towards my bedroom and office, I see her photo on the wall and I connect with her memory.

The truth is that I prefer to remember her alive, not dead. Her spirit is much bigger than her death. I wonder where her spirit is now? Could she be floating around in the air like an angel? Is she truly free of pain now? Mom was all about piano and music. Our whole family enjoyed listening to her play the piano when I was younger. When things get stressful, listening to the greatest Chopin hits helps me relax, and calm down because it reminded me of my mom. She also loved to dance, and I must have inherited both of those loves from her. She ended up having an illness that gave her a fluctuating sensorium - the area of the brain considered responsible for receiving and integrating sensations from the outside world. At times, she was disoriented with person and time. But she did not forget how to play the piano. She lives within me now in music and in laughter and in dance.

I deeply acknowledged my pain. It does not feel so painful now. More like heart twinges; more like a nostalgic feeling. The pain allowed me to contemplate on how powerful our human connections can be. Sharing my feelings with my siblings and family helped deal with the honest truth of her physical death. Her mind intermittently left us a long time ago. She was truly a guileless and innocent woman who had a gentle soul. Now her spirit lives through her children and grandchildren, and through melodies of Chopin, Beethoven, Massenet and beautiful Filipino songs.

In my job, I have been able to use this experience of loss and pain in compassionately helping others rise above their difficult circumstances. This experience of loss and going through it can add to layers of empathy for others as we go on in our lives.

Gentle Reflective Questions

1. When did you feel the most emotional pain?
2. How truthful were you about your feelings?
3. Who helped you acknowledge your pain?
4. Where were you when you felt this pain?
5. What helped you move on from your pain?

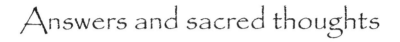

Answers and sacred thoughts

Phoenix Miracle Pearls

"The pain will leave once it has finished teaching you."

~Unknown

"One word frees us of all the weight and pain of life: the word is love."

~ Sophocles

Gentle Exercises of the Spirit

Permit ourselves to think and then whisper these thoughts three times, slowly and gently:

"I will acknowledge my pain.

There is no need to suffer.

The pain is a part of my love."

Next, imagine yourself showing kindness to someone who is hurting and in some kind of pain. What do you visualize? Think, now, about someone who you know is in pain. Think about them softly, gently and kindly. Call that person. Send a letter, text or an e-mail to that person today. Think kindly and gently as you write to this person. Then think kindly about yourself, and acknowledge your own pain.

Write a kind letter to yourself.

3. Receive help and guidance with an open heart

Many times we feel incapacitated to receive help. We may feel that by receiving help we are actually admitting to having a problem. By admitting the problem, we break through the denial that has been seemingly protecting us from a very painful truth. The truth is that disasters, losses and tragedies are a shock to our beings. They can overwhelm our psyches to a point that we don't want to believe that those occurrences are actually happening. The mind has a way of protecting itself from what seems to be hurtful. These are the times that we can choose to open up to our own vulnerabilities. Once we accept that we are human and recognize our own human frailties, it becomes much easier to receive help and guidance.

To receive help and guidance, openly, with the heart of a child is to innocently open our hearts and minds to the healing sources that surround us. There are many kinds of healing from different cultures and different parts of the world.

During an Alternative Medicine conference, I listened to a brilliant neuro-physicist speak about how he dealt with his Multiple Myeloma. He was being treated by physicians in Louisville, Kentucky. He had all the tests done and at one point there seemed to be a plateau in his treatment and care. Something in him decided to open his mind to all other types of treatment around the world. He eventually found himself in India, in a small village with friendly people. There he met a wise old man in his hut. The people in the village revered him as their wise man and he gave counsel to the people there. The neuro-physicist reported that he visited with this wise man daily in his hut where they talked about his illness and everything else. Every morning he reported that the villagers would ask him how he was doing and how his illness was. The villagers helped normalize his condition. They showed him they cared and they also asked about his illness as if that was the most normal thing. He started finding that his scientific mind had to take a rest for a while and allow the flow of the innocent way of approaching his healing. He opened his mind to whatever could heal him whether he initially believed it or not. At one point, the wise man told him that he needed to go back to Louisville and be checked by the Louisville physicians. He believed that he still had about three lesions left in his body. There was a part of the neuro-physicist that perhaps doubted his healing. Sure enough when he went back to Louisville, that was what they found.

It is not easy to just open our minds to innocently believe in our healing. We have learned so much growing up in our lives that these experiences interfere in the purity of the mind and heart in terms of what can heal us and how we can heal. Thus if we open ourselves to our healing openly with the heart of a child, the purity of our healing also manifests.

Gentle Reflective Questions

1. Who have been there for you to help you with your healing?
2. What have been your obstacles in receiving help in the past?
3. Where were you when you resisted opening up to your healing?
4. When was the last time you thought you could use some help?
5. Why do you think it is important for you to ask for help now?

Answers and sacred thoughts

Phoenix Miracle Pearls

"The wound is the place where the Light enters you"

~ Rumi

"Wherever the art of medicine is loved, there is also a love for humanity".

~ Hippocrates

Gentle Exercises of the Spirit

1. Let us sit still, close our eyes and imagine our selves being open to the energies that will help our well-being and healing. Clear our minds and focus on a soft healing light gently healing our whole body from head to toe. That healing light is going in circles slowly from our heads to our toes. Especially linger the circular motions around the areas of our bodies with pain.

2. Let us find something broken in our house. Perhaps a plate, a cup or a vase. There is a centuries old Japanese art form called "Kintsugi" also called "kinsukuroi" meaning golden repair or golden joinery. Kintsugi is the art of repairing pottery by mending the areas of breakage with powdered gold, silver or platinum. So what was once broken is now even more beautiful when repaired. Imagine ourselves in our broken and wounded parts and allowing that golden healing light to heal our wounds. As we repair our broken cup or vase or plate, imagine all that healing light restoring all our wounded parts back to health. We don't need gold or silver in this exercise. We can

be creative and we can glue what we are restoring and maybe paint something on the broken areas. Enjoy our moments of repairing with creativity. Enjoy our healing.

4. Surround ourselves with people who love us and who we love

As we grow up, we start knowing the people who we trust. We also start getting to know the people we love and who love us. As little children, our scope of loving others is mostly centered on our caregivers and those who provided for our needs. As we get older, we start learning to love others more unconditionally, whether they meet our needs or not. Eventually we learn to discern about who we love and who loves us. These people could be relatives, friends or even people who we may have only known for a short period of time but we learn to love them because of the imprint of love they have left in our hearts.

When times got tough for me, I recall calling my dad and he would answer my calls anytime of the day. As a surgeon, he was on call for his patients but he was literally on call 24/7 for our whole family, and that was including our huge extended family. My dad was a very intelligent and talented man with a huge heart who loved his family a great deal and he was a rock-solid anchor for me in times of trouble. Knowing he was there for me to talk to and discuss things was enough for me to feel secure about my own path in life.

It is important to be able to reach out to someone who you believe is a positive and hopeful influence on you. Someone who you know will either uplift your spirits or gently challenge you for the better or simply just be there with you. To have a family to support us is a wonderful thing yet if we had traumatic childhoods and experiences with our family, then it is also helpful to reach out to friends and people who have become like our emotional and spiritual families. Many times, people have been able to rely more on non-blood relatives than relatives of their own because of family dynamics.

My high school friend Gina has the uncanny ability to make me laugh no matter what the situation is. There is much love with friendships that have always been there for us. That love is shown through the lack of judgment, the unconditional support and the feeling that you know you are accepted by this person no matter what. More so, a friend who helps us laugh at ourselves and our own foibles is beyond precious. Gina is a very compassionate and kind friend who is also very bright and non-judgmental and who makes sure that she is there for you especially when times are tough. She is a fiercely loyal friend. When times were challenging and I didn't want to receive phone calls, she was the friend who would persistently call anyway and leave caring messages to make sure that I was alright. Knowing that someone cares enough to go beyond your isolating actions and persist in connecting with you is indeed a friend through and through. Gina became a chemist and she and her husband raised three incredible sons.

My children always knew who I was talking to on the phone because there would always be non-stop heart-felt laughter when talking to Gina. Like two high school teens still, we look back at every thing especially at ourselves and our own silly antics. I will talk more about this in a chapter in this book dedicated to the importance of knowing how to laugh at ourselves.

Another high school friend of mine, Yasmyne, was our brilliant valedictorian when we were in high school. She is dependable, thoughtful and loyal and would do her best to help out her friends. When we were younger, some of us used to go to her recitals as she is an excellent pianist. Yasmyne eventually became not only a physician specializing in Ophthalmology but she also went on and became a lawyer. She had done medical missions in the southern part of the Philippines. What I like about Yasmyne, as with Gina, is that we are able to talk about everything and be able to accept one another for who we are. Most of all we inherently teach one another to irreverently laugh at ourselves even in the most challenging of times.

I am so fortunate to have my elementary school and high school Prepian friends. They are forever my fountain of youth. We need friends to remind us that there are good people who care about us on our side during difficult times.

Gentle Reflective Questions

1. Who are the people who love you and who you love?
2. When do you feel the most loved by?
3. Where do you go with your loved ones that makes you happiest?
4. How do you feel when you are with loved ones?
5. What are the most loving things that your loved ones have done for you and you felt a lot of love from them?

Answers and sacred thoughts

Phoenix Miracle Pearls

"Some human beings are safe havens. Be companions with them."

~Rumi

"A friend is, as it were, a second self."

~Cicero

"Without friends, the world is but a wilderness."

~ Francis Bacon

Gentle Exercises of the Spirit

1. Imagine ourselves surrounded by the people we love and who love us.
2. If we are not with them now, get some photos of loved ones and contemplate the moments with them that gave you joy.
3. When we are with our loved ones, let us study their faces. Observe their behaviors and actions. Think about what we enjoy about them. Think about what they love about us. Relish those thoughts and feelings. Embrace the love of our loved ones. Take a deep breath. Enjoy the love they give us and the love we give them.

5. Rest. Relax. Take it easy. Conserve energy.

Many of us may find relaxing and resting difficult at times. This is especially true to those of us who tend to be very busy with activities and work that the idea of rest and relaxation becomes foreign to us. There is a time to rest and to conserve energy. Life is all about energy and at times we have to conserve some energy to replenish ourselves. Taking things easy may not be as easy especially after going through disasters, losses and tragedies.

After months of working hard, many of us look forward to going on vacations. It is not unusual that sometimes it takes a few days to actually feel relaxed because decompression is a process.

There is a transition phase between our minds working at full capacity at work, solving problems, meeting deadlines, finishing tons of paperwork, to just doing nothing. There is a change in the adrenaline flowing in our veins, much like a withdrawal or discontinuation syndrome. About two to three days is what it takes me to finally feel comfortable relaxing. At that point, I can feel my mind slow down more, my muscles relax more, my heart not beating as fast.

There is a general slowing down of our minds and bodies that eventually lead to the comfort of relaxation. There is that sense of de-stressing that helps us permit ourselves to just enjoy the present. That is usually when I start hearing the birds chirp more clearly, something that I was too busy to pay attention to previously. I even start noticing and observing their peculiar behaviors, like a blue bird flying down and sitting on one of the log pillars on the deck and just looking around.

I know I am relaxing because that is usually when I start enjoying the sun kissing my face and I start taking moments to just feel the warmth that pervades my being while the sunbeams tickle my nose. That is usually when I start feeling the wind on my hair allowing my hair to fly all around my face with glee. I love that beautiful West Wind - that gentle zephyr - that just caresses my skin and gently blows and cools my face ; that is also when I deeply enjoy inhaling that cool and tender breeze that carries the oxygen to our lungs.

When we relax, we start noticing and sensing our surroundings more. We are even able to notice the loveliness of the people around us, our families, our friends and people in general. The beauty and goodness in people seem to shine more brightly when we are relaxed. When we are stressed, the opposite seems to occur.

When feeling relaxed, we go into a state of ataraxy - a feeling of tranquility and peace - and we are able to rest our over-stimulated psyches from having to deal with the many stressors of life.

Some people talk about "being too blessed to be stressed" and they go about focusing on their many blessings instead of worrying about what may be stressors for others.

Imagine just lying on a couch, with no television or radio on, and just sensing and noticing everything around us. Then imagine that we have lavender essential oils in our diffusers filled with water and that aroma works its way to our olfactory sense and just lulls us to relaxation. How would that be? Imagine just relaxing and communing with nature and listening to the lullabies of the ocean waves? And if we are not by the ocean, we can listen to the ocean in Nature Sounds machine or we can simply imagine being by the magnificent ocean.

Traveling to places that fill our hearts with peace and joy is one of the most healing things we can do for ourselves. Many times, a change of environment is very therapeutic for us. However, if we are not able to travel, like during this coronavirus pandemic, we can certainly use our creative imaginations to fly us to the wonderful places we always dreamed about. This allows us to be mentally and emotionally transported to the places where we can take a break from life's challenges.

Gentle Reflective Questions

1. When was the last time you truly relaxed?
2. Where were you when you were able to relax?
3. Who were you with while relaxing?
4. What were you doing prior to relaxing?
5. How did you handle the transition between being busy to relaxing?

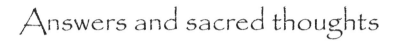

Answers and sacred thoughts

Phoenix Miracle Pearls

"How beautiful it is to do nothing, and then rest afterwards".

~ A Spanish proverb

"Our anxiety does not come from thinking about the future, but from wanting to control it."

~ Khalil Gibran

Gentle Exercises of the Spirit

1. Practice doing absolutely nothing for 15 minutes
2. Then after one week, practice doing nothing for 30 minutes
3. After that, practice doing nothing for 15 to 30 minutes daily.

Some may say that doing nothing is actually doing something. Whatever doing nothing means to you is just fine. Enjoy doing nothing. The best ideas and insights may come out of doing nothing for a time being.

6. Meditate. Cleanse our minds. Un-clutter our hearts

Meditation is to practice using a technique - such as focusing the mind on an object, thought or activity, or mindfulness, with the goal of training the mind to have more awareness and attention to achieve a mentally clear and stable mind. Meditation can help reduce anxiety and stress in many situations. There are many popular types of meditation and the following are some examples:

- Mindfulness meditation: to be mindful is to be fully aware of the present. This form of meditation helps us take utmost experience of the the "here and now" without any judgment. With this meditation, we train our minds to be tranquil and release negative thoughts.
- Spiritual meditation: this form of meditation is very similar to focused and fervent prayer. In this form of meditation we reflect on the silence around to search for a profound connection with God, a Higher Power or the universe. The goal is to get in touch with our spiritual selves.
- Loving-kindness meditation: this meditation is about cultivating our sense of kindness, compassion, good will and benevolence towards others. The practice of this meditation is beneficial in enhancing a person's self-acceptance of self and that of others.

- Mantra meditation: Mantra meditation is uttering a word, a syllable or a phrase repeatedly during meditation. In Sanskrit, "man" signifies the "mind" and "tra" means release.
- Transcendental meditation: TM is a form of silent mantra meditation that was developed by Maharishi Mahesh Yogi. In TM, we close our eyes, take a few deep breaths, and use the mantra for 20 minutes twice a day. We repeat the mantra in our minds.

Each one of us can explore various forms of meditation and find those that are most comfortable for us.

Many people from the Orient grew up with the concept of meditation. Meditation has been helpful in that the mind, heart and body can improve with regular meditation. It has been written that meditation can ease anxiety, stress, boost moods and immunity, and ease chronic pain. When people meditate, they are better able to set aside some of the negative sensations produced by anxiety and stress. Reduction of stress is one of the main indications of meditation. It follows that with less feelings of stress, then anxiety is lowered.

Meditation can also enhance self-awareness. As we get rid of our mind-clutter, the mind finds it much easier to acquire deep insights about ourselves and the situations we have chosen to be in. Meditation has also been known to lengthen attention span and may decrease age-related memory loss. It has also been utilized in addictions treatment. People who meditate may feel a sense of calmness and tranquility of spirit that could also help in cultivating kindness towards others.

During disaster relief work in Thailand while serving the people affected by the tsunami, it was so calming to the spirit just to observe the ever-present monks in their flowing orange robes walking around quietly. Their meditative presence gently gave us a sense of peace in the midst of the aftermath of the tsunami. Their walking meditation made them appear as if they were floating on air as they walked. They appeared to me as if they were like angels on earth with a lightness in their beings. The monks exuded a calming presence that was much needed in the midst of devastation.

During a break from tsunami relief work, my Thai friends took me to meet the abbott in a monastery. The abbott was meditating with more than three hundred inmates. They were very calm and very focused on their chanting and meditation. During the meditative moments, there was profound silence and peace. Later on, I was allowed to speak with some of the inmates with my translators. They told me about their life stories and the losses and tragedies that they had gone through. Many of them said that their meditation helped them deal with being away from their families and loved ones. They reported that they were able to focus on more positive things about their own lives.

While in meditation, our minds tend to become uncluttered from all distractions, allowing us a more synchronized and focused way of thinking. When we un-clutter our minds, this helps un-clutter our hearts by getting rid of anger, resentments and despair.

Without the excess baggage of emotional and mental clutter, it becomes much easier to apply all our coping skills in dealing with our dilemma. This can help us figure out ways to deal with our problems by lessening the unnecessary distractions that tend to overwhelm our minds.

However, meditation is not for everybody. In some situations, it may be necessary to talk to a therapist or psychiatrist regarding the value of meditation in terms of one's well-being.

Gentle Reflective Questions

1. What is your understanding about meditation?
2. When do you feel that meditation can benefit you?
3. What time of day is best for you to meditate?
4. Why do you believe that meditation may help you?
5. Where do you think is your best place/places to meditate?

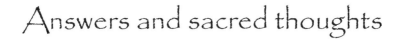

Answers and sacred thoughts

Phoenix Miracle Pearls

"The inspiration you seek is already within you. Be silent and listen."

~ Rumi

"Calmness of mind is one of the beautiful jewels of wisdom."

~ James Allen

Gentle Exercises of the Spirit

1. Let us allow ourselves to just sit quietly under a tree, or in a comfortable place in our home. Wear loose clothing, nothing too tight nor fitting. Allow our mind, body and being to breathe. Slowly and gently caress and stroke our head, face, arms, abdomen and then our legs all the way down to our feet. Think kindly of ourselves.

2. Then very slowly take a deep breath through your nose and then out of your mouth. Let us do this three times in a very gradual, calmly prolonged and slow manner.

3. We will now sit in and take on a position that is comfortable for us. Many sit in the lotus position for meditation. We may want to sit on a pillow or just right on a rug or a mat on the floor. Our hands will lay gently on our knees or with our thumbs and middle fingers touching each other.

4. Let us then focus our minds on a peaceful and happy time in our lives. This could be recent or way in the past. Everyone of us has different "comfort thoughts" and "blissful times" in our lives. If any difficulties focusing, then repeat the breaths three times. Be mindful of

each breath we take and relish that fresh air slowly going into our nostrils all the way down to our lungs. Then gently exhale and let go. Enjoy the moments of peace and tranquility.

7. Pray. On our knees. In the midst of nature. *Everywhere*

To pray is to choose to communicate and connect with a higher source. Prayer is the divine communication between a person and the god of their understanding. Prayer is a focused positive energy towards others as when parents pray for the well-being and safety of their children. People have their favorite prayer places. Christians are taught that Jesus prayed in the Garden of Gethsemane. Muslims have their special prayer mats and they pray five times daily. Native Americans talk about "walking in prayer" whereby a person is in a continuous communication with the Creator.

I personally love praying while communing with nature. My home has many windows all around and I feel fortunate and blessed to be able to relish the view of the beautiful Black Hills wherever I walk anywhere at home. So when I am doing routine chores at home, I tend to "walk in prayer" and quietly commune with God about my everyday happenings and about family, friends and our world. After having gone through losses, disasters and tragedies, I pray to be a more loving, compassionate and kinder person. Many times, it is not easy to be all of that when there are challenging circumstances. Most of my prayers have to do with gratitude for everything, for everyone, for all the love and kindness I've received all my life. I pray for all the many blessings I have experienced in our ephemeral lives.

For many years, Lawrence and I have flown back and forth to New York City, the Big Apple, the pulse of the world, to visit family. We make it a point to visit St. Patrick's Cathedral on 5th Avenue and 50th Street to pray and light candles for loved ones. Many times, we sit on the pews and just remain silent in prayer, or we kneel as we pray. The reverberating echoes inside the walls of this magnificent Gothic cathedral heighten the sense of sacredness within.

Back in the Pine Ridge reservation and at one point, here in the Black Hills, Lawrence ran his sweat lodges. Lawrence is Native American Lakota and was a sun dancer for almost thirty years. The Lakota spirituality is quite profound in the way prayers are sent to God through the sweat lodge. The heat from the hot rocks make us sweat and cleanse ourselves in body and spirit as we pray to our Creator.

When I was young, my family prayed and said the rosary together. There is something about "a family that prays together, stays together". My grandmother always told us that. I remember one of my grandmothers, while watching the pope on television, remarked that she wished that we could all go and pray in the Vatican while the pope was giving mass.

Lawrence and I stayed for a few days in Rome, Italy before and after a Mediterranean cruise. Rome was simply amazing and walking around there felt like we were right in the middle of our history books, recognizing many of the historical structures which were part of the grandeur of the Roman Empire. On a sunny Sunday morning, we walked towards the Vatican and the area was so crowded with people from all over the world. So we decided to not go in because what appeared to be the impossibility of the long lines going into the Vatican.

The next day, we chose to walk to the Roman Forum and the Colosseum area of Rome and marveled at the cobble stones everywhere. Walking around is something we enjoy so we walked practically all day long until it was about 4 PM that day. I really don't know what got into me but all of a sudden, I felt compelled to go back to the Vatican with Lawrence. At that point, I just couldn't imagine being in Rome and for Lawrence not to see the Sistine Chapel and the inside of the Vatican. Needless to say, I talked to Lawrence about walking back to the Vatican which was practically on the other side of the city. I told him that I just had this feeling that we needed to go there and it may or may not be open. One of the things that I love about Lawrence is that he was always ready to support my strong internal feelings of doing things. He just gave me a look of understanding and without any questions nor discussions said, "Let's go". We unconditionally respected each others intuition and no explanations required.

So, there we were, walking back a long way on the cobble stones and finally got to the Vatican. We were glad to see that it was still open and there were only about a dozen people in line. By the time it was our turn to get in, the Vatican guard told us that we couldn't go in. With a sense of frustration and consternation, especially because we had walked from such a distance just to get there, I pleaded with the guard in broken Italian to please let us in. He still said no so, finally I asked, "Is there anything else open for us to see?". So he said "Yes, the church is open". So I happily told him that the church was exactly where we wanted to go. Evidently, it was the museum that was already closed.

Entering the Vatican church, one can easily feel that Catholic reverence that I grew up with. The tall ceilings, the incredible paintings, the echoes from every sound and words that we spoke. Our awe was written all over our faces with our eyes absorbing everything we were seeing at that time. It was Monday then and there were hardly any people there, which was great. As we were taking photographs, suddenly, we heard the whispers and susurrus of people behind us. They were speaking in various languages. But then I heard someone say "Papa!". The guards started pushing the mid-waist railings to back off the people as a procession started. Lawrence kept taking photos of the procession and sure enough, there was the distinct papal mitre - a tall folded hat that has a top that looks like a fish's mouth. As I was hopping up and down so I could see better, I noticed that the guards, allowed a couple of ladies in and I overheard the older lady say in Italian that they were just wanting to attend the mass. After seeing that they would allow people in, I put down my camera back in to my purse and held Lawrence's hand and told the guard that we just also wanted to go to mass. And lo and behold, they let us in!

We were all in a small circular chapel area of the Vatican. Pope Francis "Papa Francesco" was leading the mass. I am not sure exactly what happened to me but I started thinking about my grandmother and what she said about being in the Vatican, and here we were. It was as if the Holy Spirit went through me and tears just started rolling down my cheeks. In my heart, my grandmother's spirit was right there with us. In my spirit, I was so grateful to God to be right there at that time and living my grandmother's prayer to be in the Vatican.

Pope Francis' sermon was about his calling and how he felt compelled to follow that special and distinct call. He is known as the "people's pope" for his humility and his ability to relate with people with kindness and compassion. On top of it all, Pope Francis was the one who gave us communion.

We walked out of the Vatican that night filled with the Spirit. What an unbelievable and wonderful spiritual experience we had. It was all so unexpected and unplanned. In my heart, I prayed for our families and all our loved ones who had gone before us. I prayed for those who are suffering disasters, losses and tragedies and for those who struggled with physical, emotional and spiritual ailments. I prayed to God and thanked God for this beautiful experience on earth; these moments of connectedness to our Highest Source. Lawrence had felt the same exact spiritual feeling.

As tired as both of us were from walking all day long, we felt so fresh and rejuvenated after we got out of the Vatican. All our aches and pains from all day walking were miraculously gone or at least, we couldn't feel any pain. It was as if our spirits were cleansed and purified and our physical ailments that day just disappeared. I wondered if this was similar to what people feel when they have spontaneous remissions from their illnesses when they take their pilgrimages to places of faith like the Lourdes in France. Faith is powerful.

My most profound prayers, I have prayed in a sweat lodge. In the Lakota sweat lodge, the one that Lawrence ran, the most important thing is the spirituality and our way of believing in the Creator as we understand the Creator. People are welcome regardless of their religion because in essence, praying in a sweat lodge is about our own understanding of our relationship with our Creator. I like the encompassing nature of praying in the sweat lodge and we always end our prayers with *Mitakuye Oyasin,* that we are all interconnected. In other words, I can remain being Catholic in religion and still be accepted to pray in the sweat lodge to cultivate my own choice of relating with our Creator (*Tunkasila*).

Prayer helps us stay connected with our Creator and with that, anything is possible. If anything is possible, then all healing is possible.

Gentle Reflective Questions

1. Who did you pray with? If you don't pray, who did you think positive thoughts about? When was the last time you prayed? When was the last time you thought positively about others?
2. What did you pray about? What were your positive thoughts about?
3. Where do you feel most comfortable praying? Where do you feel comfortable thinking positive thoughts about others?
4. Why do you pray / or not pray?
5. When have you ever felt compelled to do something unplanned and things ended up miraculously beautiful?

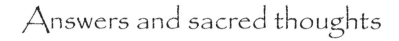

Answers and sacred thoughts

Phoenix Miracle Pearls

"Pray for my soul. More things are wrought by prayer than this world dreams of: wherefore, let their voice, rise like a fountain for me night and day."

~ Alfred Lord Tennyson

"Prayer does not change God, but it changes him who prays"

~ Soren Kierkegaard

Gentle Exercises of the Spirit

1. Let us practice praying at home for 10 minutes straight to the God of our understanding. If we do not believe in God or are agnostic, think about people we would like to send positive thoughts to.

2. Let us practice praying while in the midst of nature. Perhaps this could be when we are out walking in a park or hiking. Or maybe even when we are sitting watching an ocean, a sea, a river, a lake, or a little brook in your area.

3. Let us practice praying when it is hard to pray for whatever reason

4. Let us practice "walking in prayer". Let us stay in communication with the God of our understanding for a period of time.

8. Stay humble

When we contemplate about how relatively small we are batted against the whole universe, we realize that humility comes from being aware of the concept of relativity. When we look at the stars and see the expanse of the skies, we start realizing that there exists a Highest Force out there that created all of what seems to be an infinite vastness that no human alone could have created.

That thought can keep us humble. That we are but a speck in the bigger scheme of things in this universe allows us to set aside our egos.

Being humble can mean that we accept that we don't know everything even though we may have learned a lot. In my book *The Courage to Encourage* I wrote about the wisdom and humility of Socrates whereby he addressed the idea that the more he knew, the more he didn't know. When we choose to continue to learn no matter how we feel we have become experts in certain fields, choosing to keep an open mind to learn keeps us humble.

In Psychiatry, the interviews during psychiatric evaluations are socratic in nature. To get to know someone, we have to ask questions and not assume. To ask questions means that we don't know, so we are asking as we are interested in understanding people to be able to serve them in some way. There is utmost humility in not knowing, yet wanting to learn about another person.

I have known many people who I considered humble from all walks of life. One of them was a colleague and friend, a very wise man from India, Dr. Pran Ravani. When he came to work, he wore simple work attires and he had a kind and gentle demeanor about him. Pran was called "bapu" or spiritual father by some of his Indian friends and colleagues. He became a very good friend and taught me a lot about how to listen and hear people at the same time, and how to relax power struggles with patients and people in general.

Dr. Ravani was a sage in defusing conflictual situations by simply and masterfully putting aside his ego in the service of his patient. There is an underlying sense of humility in this. It has to do with putting our own interests to rest while validating what another person may want us to understand. To relax a power struggle means to let go of our own judgmental opinions to accommodate what another persons thoughts and ideas are about. Sometimes it means to take a one-down position to validate someone else without losing our core values or sense of integrity.

At first glance, because of the humble way of presenting his appearance, one would think that Dr. Ravani may be having some financial strain. One of my other colleagues even wondered if we needed to chip in to buy him a suit for some medical gala. So what a surprise when we found out from another friend of his that they also called him the "silver king" of his region in India. He used what he earned to help his family and many people in his village in India.

People in India respectfully called Mathama Gandhi "bapu" - father of the Indian Nation. So being called "bapu" was a high level of respect for this very humble man.

Humility in people is manifested in many different ways. It cuts across religions, cultures and socioeconomic status, since there very humble people among the poor and the rich. Humility is a special way of being able to allow others to feel valued while not putting much attention to our own achievements or egos.

Humility is considered a virtue. Being humble is about how much difference we can make in the lives of others, and not how important we can become. Being humble means to be someone who is without an excess of pride. Believing that we can learn something from others is part of humility. If we tend to brag about being humble, we may have too much pride about being humble to actually be humble. This is called "humble-bragging". There is also false humility, for instance, when we try to deflect praise which we truly deserve or when we fish for compliments to draw attention to ourselves.

In an era where "selfies" are popular and part of a global norm, we have the story of a Lakota Native American warrior and hero named Chief Crazy Horse who was well known for his leadership, bravery and quiet humility. He did not want anyone to take his photograph so there is no known photograph of Crazy Horse though there are claims about some photographs of him. Crazy Horse (*Tasunke Witko*) was one of the Sioux leaders who defeated George Armstrong Custer's seventh cavalry at the battle of Big Horn in the Montana Territory in 1876. He was known to have been committed to upholding and safeguarding the traditions and principles of the Lakota way of life.

John Neihardt, the author of the book *Black Elk Speaks* described Crazy Horse as a man of great humility who was generous to the poor, the elderly, and children. Joseph Marshall III, in his book *The Journey of Crazy Horse: A Lakota History*, underscored Crazy horse's humility and wrote about how he was a quiet, shy and humble man who mainly worried about the less fortunate among his people. Humility is about thinking about others more than we think about ourselves. In this sense, humility is about the manner in which we put aside our needs for the benefit of others.

When we stay humble, when we focus on other people first before our selves, this can help us heal from our disasters, losses and tragedies. When we are humble we embrace the fact that we are all human and that we are all no better nor worse than others. By staying humble, we lessen the load that our egos sometimes impose upon us. Being humble allows us to be better connected with others and thus, others can relate much easier with us as opposed to when we are full of ourselves with our egos at the helm of our actions. To be humble is to know our foibles and our flaws. It is not to say that humility is humiliation. There is nothing humiliating about being humble. On the contrary, being humble is to accept our sense of humanity and in so doing we are able to connect with other people more; whereas, our grandiose hubris tends to disconnect us from others. When we are humble, we don't have that inner conflict nor pressure of having to prove ourselves to others. That relaxes our spirits and thus helps us stay much more serene which can help in our healing.

Interestingly, as humble as Crazy Horse was known to be, a Crazy Horse Memorial- the largest mountain carving in the world - where his head and his horse were carved on a mountain here in the Black Hills by sculptor Korczak Ziolkowski, was started in 1948. His huge family and supporters are continuing this project into fruition whereby the monument will be 641 feet long and 563 feet high.

I have a couple of thoughts. It seems the more humble people are, the easier for others to uplift one's essence and virtues. And my last thought? I wonder what Crazy Horse, a humble warrior would think about his massive monument, knowing that he did not even want to have his photograph taken?

Gentle Reflective Questions

1. What other qualities do you see in a humble person?
2. Who are exemplars of humility for you?
3. When did you get in touch with your sense of humility?
4. Where were you when you observed some humble people?
5. Why is humility a valued virtue?
6. How do you know if you are truly humble?

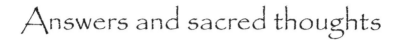

Answers and sacred thoughts

Phoenix Miracle Pearls

"To lead the people, walk behind them"

~ Lao Tzu

"The only true wisdom is knowing you know nothing"

~ Socrates

Gentle Exercises of the Spirit

1. Think of a time when we were in the presence of a humble person.
   Describe why we thought that this person was humble.
2. Think of a time when we thought that we acted humbly.
   Describe our actions during that time.
3. Think of how it felt when we chose to act humbly and put aside our ego just to promote peace.
   Describe how that felt for us.
4. Practice mindfulness about humility when our instinct may be to put our egos in the forefront. Reflect on how that felt like when we practiced humility instead of imposing our pride on others.

9. Be kind and gentle to ourselves and others

Many of us are very hard on ourselves. I tell people that they can not be harder on me than I am with myself. This requires the balance of learning to be kind and gentle with ourselves. As we learn to be kinder to ourselves, we somehow also find it easier to be kinder to others. Perhaps the other way around also works. Choosing to be kind to others may also help us be kind to ourselves.

In the process of healing, it is important that we start healing ourselves by treating ourselves kindly. This may be difficult for some people who are used to blaming themselves, those who feel guilty about things, or those who have been so used to being mistreated or abused. It can be tough for those who have self-imposed sense of obligations that being kind to oneself is an uncomfortable and unfamiliar feeling for them. If we have difficulties being kind to ourselves, then perhaps some therapy or counseling can help us understand ourselves more.

During my residency training, one of my clinical supervisors focused on this aspect in one of our supervisions. In Psychiatry, it is imperative that we are aware of our own issues so that we can navigate transferences and counter-transferences for the benefit of our patients. The concepts of "Physician know thyself" and "Physician heal thyself" are more than significant in our work with people. Though we pose to create a golden thread of connection with our patients, it is important to be aware of what we are transmitting to our patients in a psychodynamic way. The idea is to create healthy therapeutic boundaries whereby we know what our issues are and we understand what our patients' issues are. In this way, we are much more able to give kindness, empathy and compassion towards our patients without taking their behaviors personally. We remind ourselves that our patients are there because they need help regarding their mental health problems that have overwhelmed and affected their lives.

In Substance Use treatment, we use some confrontation awareness of our addicted patients' behaviors that have been destructive in their lives and their loved ones' lives. In the treatment of people with addictions, we focus on the behaviors without judging the person.

Kindness can be shown in many different ways. Family members who tend to enable the loved one who has addictions may think that they are being kind to the addict by giving them their alcohol or denying their loved ones addiction. Alcoholics Anonymous has been very helpful in imbuing hope to our addicts through the wisdom of the 12-steps and fellowship through the AA meetings.

In Al-Anon meetings, family members learn how to detach with love from the addict's behaviors. People learn in those meetings that kindness towards our addicted loved one is not about enabling their actions. Actually enabling is deemed to be unkind as it just foments the addicts' addiction and progression of their destructive behaviors. In other words, kindness may be a version of "tough love" and may not be as gentle as we would like to be.

When we tend to be too hard on ourselves, this creates pressure within our spirits which consequently make it difficult for us to heal from certain situations. If we think of life as a series of learning experiences rather than a series of mistakes, we are able to heal more. Healing also means taking responsibility for our actions and hopefully, we learn to focus more on our emotional and mental health rather than the actions that led us astray from our healthy selves.

Gentle Reflective Questions

1. Who are the people who have been kind to you?
2. When did you have feelings of kindness and compassion for others?
3. Where were you when you received kindness from others?
4. What led for you to feel kindness to others who normally evoked frustration within you?
5. How did you get to the point of being kind to yourself and/or others?

Answers and sacred thoughts

Phoenix Miracle Pearls

"Kindness in words creates confidence. Kindness in thinking creates profoundness. Kindness in giving creates love."

~ Lao Tzu

"Compassion is love's passion."

~ author

Gentle Exercises for the Spirit

1. Practice speaking kindly to ourselves in our minds. Learn to lower our voices when we speak in a kind tone towards others.

2. Keep practicing lowering the tone of our voice when speaking with others.

3. Do a random act of kindness for someone. Perhaps we might want to send someone a card to tell them that they are in our thoughts. Call someone who we have not spoken to for a while. Kindly be interested in how they are doing. Tell someone that they are important to us and that we value them. Honestly and kindly compliment someone about something that we love or like about them. Praise your children for their good hearts.

4. Keep practicing random acts of kindness for others daily. Remember to treat ourselves kindly.

10. Nurture quiet times. Silence.

Quiet times and silence can be very healing. It allows us to still our minds from the barrage of external stimulations of every day life. Life can get noisy and to heal it is important to find those golden quiet moments to get back to our center. This is a time when we consciously make an effort to just focus on healing ourselves.

Silence can truly be golden though not all the time. There are times when silence can be detrimental like when a person has been abused and could not speak up because of threats by the abuser. In this case, to be silent is to perpetuate being victimized by an abuser.

One of the most incredible silent moments I experienced was watching twenty tai-chi masters practice tai-chi right on the street in Louisville, Kentucky. The silence was so profound and still that one could hear a pin drop. Watching them go through those graceful, balanced and slow dance-like motions added a sense of sacredness and serenity as they moved from one tai-chi step to another.

The practice of tai-chi allows me to slow down more and be more mindful of my thoughts, words and actions. Many times in between seeing my patients I do a combination of some tai-chi moves as well as yoga stretches. It allows me to be still and quiet in my mind and thus I feel refreshed and able to go on to my next patients with serenity. These moments of silence allow us to clear our thoughts without distractions. In many ways, silence allows our brains to rest.

The coronavirus pandemic required us to maintain social distancing for our protection and that of others, and this led to people having some quiet times. Some people ended up appreciating these silent and quiet moments in that they were able to indulge in more creative activities. For people who are used to noise it is a different story. Some people are used to noise and thus silence can be uncomfortable for them.

As we choose to withdraw from the chatter and noise, we can gradually ease ourselves into the tranquility of silence. Therein we can find the center of our quiet solitude.

When people are in grief, or struggle with post-traumatic stress because of losses, disasters or tragedies, moments of silence can be very healing. It can soothe the rawness of the mind from all the trauma that one may have experienced by giving the mind a quiet respite.

Silence may not be completely silent or without some sounds. Many times silence can be with gentle soothing music or with the calming rhythms of poetry.

More than listen

Listen to the silence, of our forgiving hearts
Do we hear the tender melodies
Reverberating within our souls?
Do we feel the gentleness of times before
When the vital waters of Mother Earth's womb
Infused our divine celestial spirits
to be born free with the will to choose?

Listen to the echoes of the winds
Of untold memories that have lingered
the beautiful vignettes of passion
that immersed our innocent lives
as together we journeyed
Are we hearing the longing of the spirits
To unite with all, the golden connections
Our Creator has gifted to us all?

Listen to the joy and exuberance
Do we hear the meadowlark
As it flies across the magnificent
pastel colors of the break of dawn?
Are we hearing the hummingbird's
fluttering wings?
as it savors the nectar of life
Can we hear the voices in our hearts
connected with love and compassion?

Listen to the sound of Nature and Life
Of feeling blessed with solid truth
And the mystery of Love
that resides within our beings
Did we listen to our hearts?
Did we hear the music of our soul's delights?
Did we follow our heart's paths?
to our spiritual best
Did we listen to the silence?
Did we hear it all?
Before, now and after
Eternally, faithfully and beautifully
Forevermore

Gentle Reflective Questions

1. When was the last time you had a truly quiet time?
2. What were your thoughts when you had silence around you?
3. Where is the best place for you to find silence?
4. Who do you enjoy silence with?
5. Why do you think silence is important?

Answers and sacred thoughts

Phoenix Miracle Pearls

"Listen to silence. It has so much to say"

~ Rumi

"The quieter you become the more you are able to hear".

~ Rumi

Gentle Exercises of the Spirit

1. Find a quiet place. It can be in your home or in nature.
2. Just sit and be still for a while. Unplug. No cellphones.
3. What do you see? What do you hear? What do you sense?
4. Close your eyes and listen to the silence? How do you feel?

11. Allow ourselves to cry. Allow ourselves to smile.

There are times when it is hard to cry. After a tragedy, loss or disaster, we start to feel numb. Our minds are still trying to accommodate all that happened to us. The tears don't fall because our minds are still protecting us from feeling completely overwhelmed and as we get some bearing, the painful situations start hitting us. Our denial starts to loosen up and out comes the emotions like a river flowing. This is usually when the tears just come rolling down our faces. Some of us who are caregivers try to be stoic so we can stay strong for our loved ones affected by losses and tragedies.

We have this notion that to cry may be perceived as showing weakness at a time when strength is necessary. Yet there is nothing weak in showing our real and authentic emotions. In fact, being authentic and real is pure strength. To cry is to cleanse our souls and our hearts from what hurt us. To cry is to release the intense pressures of our spirits when situations cause us pain. So if we have to cry buckets to heal, then cry we must.

Some say that tears are prayers too. Every tear drop that falls on our cheeks is a liquid form of the love we have for our loved one who passed away.

When a tragedy befell our family, I cried buckets. I felt relief after that. Like I unloaded my pain through those tears. As time passes, just when we think that we may not be able to smile again, we start smiling. In the beginning, our smiles, may even seem awkward. There is a part of us that may even feel guilty smiling or feeling any kind of joy. Some of us may even feel disrespectful to our deceased loved ones, if we start feeling moments of joy. In reality, our loved ones would want us not to suffer. They would want us to find a way to get back to our lives and our dreams. Our loved ones would surely want us to be resilient and move on towards all that we hoped to do in our earthy lives. Each one of us has a different timing when it comes to healing.

When we allow ourselves to finally smile or even laugh again, we know that we are allowing the process of grief to gradually pass though us. That means that we are permitting ourselves to go back to ourselves and embrace all our human emotions again besides grief. Grief can be a mixture of feelings, from sadness to anger to despondence. However, when we can allow ourselves to smile again, we get back in touch with the lightness of our beings that can help with our healing.

Gentle Reflective Questions

1. Where were you when you started crying?
2. Who were you with when your tears started to fall?
3. When was the time that you felt like crying?
4. What caused you to cry?
5. How did you start smiling again? What happened that made you smile after your grief?

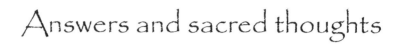

Answers and sacred thoughts

Phoenix Miracle Pearls

"There is a sacredness in tears. They are not the mark of weakness but of power. They speak more eloquently than ten thousand tongues. They are the messengers of overwhelming grief, of deep contrition, and of unspeakable love."

~ Washington Irving

"Tears come from the heart and not from the brain."

~ Leonardo da Vinci

Gentle Exercises for the Spirit

1. Think about when we cried watching a movie. What were we feeling at that time? What do we think triggered us to cry? What did the movie remind us of?
2. Think about when we cried with someone. What were we feeling then?
3. Think about the first time we ever smiled after a period of grief?
   Describe what it felt like when we first smiled again.

12. Start looking at what wounded us with clarity

It is not an easy task to take a look at who and what has wounded us. Many people prefer to look away from what happened to them for fear of feeling - re-traumatized. Therapy is a way of healing so we look at our past like a participant observer of the circumstances we went through, only to learn from them. We take care not to dwell in the past so we can enjoy our present and we can dream about our future.

When we think about the person or the situation that has wounded us, we may do so with some hesitation. It may regress us back to feeling the hurt we may have felt or the loss we may have experienced. We begin to understand that what happened led us to where we are now in our lives.

When pondering about the losses I've suffered, there was an initial resistance to accept what happened. It may feel so much easier to deny the pain we experienced. No one ever wants to lose a loved one. No one ever wants to be hurt in any way by anyone.

Once we make a choice to look at what happened in our lives with clarity, and this in itself is a process, we start seeing our lives as a journey of learning experiences. We are then able to take the good with the bad and start to realize that our lives are extraordinary journeys that eventually lead us to hopefully be our best selves. What have we learned from all that happened to us? How can these situations help us evolve into the individuals we hope to be?

The Serenity Prayer: *"God, grant me the serenity, to accept the things I can not change, to change the things I can, and the wisdom to know there difference."* There are many things that are not under our control. It is futile and a head-banger to try to control the things that we truly are unable to control.

Our realization of our powerlessness over people, places and things, lead us to humbly face the circumstances in our lives with more clarity and acceptance. We need to overcome our denial of who or what hurt us to get to the point where we can eventually make positive changes for ourselves. We can control the way we respond to our trials and tribulations better once we have clarity and when we can accept that we have no control over others.

When we look at who or what has wounded us with clarity, it does not mean that we will tolerate being hurt over and over again. We can not live our lives continually seeing ourselves as victims. We all have the God-spark of power within that would help us heal, rise and soar from human devastations. This is what the Phoenix Miracle is all about.

Once we accept the truth that we were hurt, then we can position ourselves so we are not hurt again and we can respond with courage and strength to help us heal our wounds.

Gentle Reflective Questions

1. Who do you feel has hurt you in the past? How did you deal with this hurt?
2. What happened that led to the hurt?
3. When did you feel a loss? When did you feel wounded and hurt?
4. Why was it difficult to let go of the hurt? What is the worst thing that could happen if we accept the things we cannot change? What are things that we could proactively change?

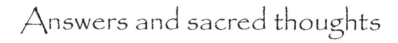

Answers and sacred thoughts

Phoenix Miracle Pearls

"Acceptance of what has happened is the first step to overcoming the consequences of any misfortune.""

~ William James

"The moment you accept what troubles you have been given, the door will open".

~ Rumi

Gentle Exercise for the Spirit

1. Imagine briefly and fleetingly a situation that hurt us. It could be a loss, it could be a break-up. It could be a tragedy. Then go back to the present and see how far we've come. What did we learn looking back? Did what we learn help us be more resilient in current situations that are challenging?
2. Imagine a situation that truly gave us joy. Stay in this situation for a while. Feel what made us joyful. Remember the situations that made us feel blessed and loved. Linger our thoughts during this situation and now bring it to the present with us. How does it feel?

13. Prepare to rise.

There is a powerful healing energy that eventually propels us to rise up.

As we heal from disasters, losses and tragedies, somewhere within us, rises the energy of growth and resilience. If we've ever seen a soft green plant crack through hard rocks just to grow, that is the vision that I have in this stage of healing.

Within us is that immutable, natural longing to heal and to evolve. This is the phase where we begin to feel that inner energy that had decreased during grief and loss. It is almost a feeling of rebirth and no different from a caterpillar about ready to rise to become a beautiful butterfly.

After a period of grief, the time has come to break free from the shackles of despair. We need to be able to embrace this period in our lives to move on to the next stages in our healing.

Let Us Rise

Let us rise
to the beat
of our inner drums
Rise to the beauty
of our souls within

Let us rise
to praise the strength
of our humanity
Rise to the whispering
call of the universe

Let us rise
with gratitude
for everything we are
for all that we will be

Rise to the stars
with hands outstretched
to embrace our lives
with abundance blessed.

Let us rise, let us rise
to our very best.

~ author

Gentle Reflective Questions

1. Who do you envision to be with when we start rising?
2. What feelings do we have as we rise?
3. When do we think is a good time to rise up from our grief and loss?
4. Where is a good place for us to rejoice in our rising?
5. Why is it important to imagine how life would be if we allow ourselves to rise?

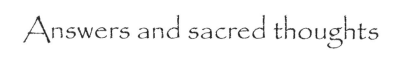

Answers and sacred thoughts

Phoenix Miracle Pearls

"Let us rise beyond any trials or tribulations and know that we are all interconnected by our love and our compassion."

~ author~

"Our inner strength lies in our ability to rise up and uplift others to be their very best selves."

~ author~

Gentle Exercises for the Spirit

1. Read Maya Angelou's poem - Still I Rise.
   What thoughts came into our minds as we read the poem?
2. What does rising above life's challenges and adversities mean to us?
3. Imagine our selves rising up in a hot air balloon? How do we feel?
   What do we see? What would we like to see?

WE RISE

1. Breathe. Breathe deeply. Inhale the fresh air.

Going outside on the deck, taking deep breaths of fresh air and seeing the beauty of the Black Hills, gives me inner joy in the morning. Inhaling fresh air cleanses our lungs and allows us to initiate that air flow within us to start our day. All that pure oxygen we breathe aids our circulation. Contemplating on inhaling and exhaling fresh air allows us to feel how alive we are and thus we can embrace each day more mindfully.

It has been too easy for us to take our breaths for granted. Breathing normally happens automatically so we breathe semiconsciously. Yet let us imagine, treating each breath with respect and attention. One breath at a time, leads us to remember how important life is and how interconnected we are with air. It reminds us to keep our environments unpolluted so we can continue to enjoy that beautiful fresh air.

One breath, just one single breath is what divides life from death. Both my dad and my sister died in my arms and I was there for their very last breath. Those heartbreaking moments of loss magnified the significance of what one breath means. No breath, no life.

The tragic death of George Floyd inspired many people from all different races from all over the world to stand up and protest against injustice. Prior to his death, he repeatedly stated "I can't breathe." People everywhere can relate to the significance of not being able to breathe.

In the hubbub of life, many times, we take for granted the importance of breathing. It is for this reason that many spiritual yogi teach us to focus on our breaths. Each breath reminds us how precious life is. Every breath teaches us not to take our lives for granted. Each breath reminds us to enjoy every moment. Every breath we take helps us value the beautiful exchange we have with nature. We learn to be grateful for the lungs of our earth - our life-giving trees and plants.

For our healing we need to remember to breathe in that wonderful fresh air, the powerful life force that heals us. Each breath matters.

Gentle Reflective Questions

1. What does breathing mean to you?
2. Where do you go to take breaths of fresh air?
3. Why do you think it is important to be mindful of our breaths?
4. Who do you think about when you take some fresh air?
5. When will you start breathing practices?

Answers and sacred thoughts

Phoenix Miracles Pearls

"When you arise in the morning, think of what a precious privilege it is to be alive, to breathe, to think, to enjoy, and to love."

~ Marcus Aurelius

"To know even one life has breathed easier because you have lived. This is to have succeeded."

~ Ralph Waldo Emerson

Gentle Exercises for the Spirit

1. Let's go outside and breathe some fresh air. Let's just relax and inhale through our noses, very slowly, and then ever so gradually exhale out of our mouths. Let us do this five times, the slower the better. Then let us feel how that fresh air travels through our noses all the way into our lungs. Feel how the air cools us from the nose to the lungs. Every breath is important. It reminds us to value our lives and live in the breath; live in the present moment. There is no other time but now.

2. Let us remember and think of how important our lives are. Let us also remember how important others' lives are.
    Let us breathe in compassion, love, kindness, gratitude and basic goodness that we feel in the air. Let us breathe in all the miraculous possibilities that our lives will bring. Let us breathe and celebrate our lives, that we may follow our life purpose and be the best that we can be.

2. Find alone times. Not lonely times. Learn something new.

Solitude can be very healing. The coronavirus pandemic certainly put us in situations of social distancing and solitude. This solitude can be very healthy for all of us. We can choose to cultivate our creativity and find time to do the things that we did not have much time to do in the past. While in solitude, it allows us to concentrate more on what keeps us peaceful, stable and happy. For me, I am able to write more freely when I am alone. This is also a time when I play my musical instruments more. We can still be connected with others while in solitude through texts, calls and social media. But that remains limited. Alone, we are able to think more clearly without the interruption of other people's dialogues. We are able to focus on the things that we always hoped we could do if we only had our time alone.

When I was younger, I always wondered how the monks and the nuns in the convents survive such cloistered lives. In solitude, they are able to pray more and strengthen their relationship with their highest source without distractions.

There is a reason why retreats have been very helpful to our well-being. There are times when we just need to have some space and time to leave out the ongoing noise that we routinely have in our lives. By doing so, we start to hear our inner thoughts and our inner insights. This is one reason why many writers need a lot of quiet times to be able to access their creative minds to come out with the words they want to write. Being in solitude does not necessarily mean that we are completely alone. We remain connected with others in our hearts and our minds. We are able to actually get better perspectives about our family, friends and life in general. Things become more crystal clear when we have our times of solitude.

Solitude is also not for everybody. Some people truly have difficulties being alone. They need constant companionship by family and friends and some need to be surrounded by people all the time. In this case, we can practice being in solitude by just merely creating a special sacred space in our homes if possible.

When we go through losses or tragedies, we end up having a sense of rawness in our beings. Some of us may even be like open emotional wounds. Just like any physical wound, we want to give it time to heal. We want the wound to be left alone without being touched because it may lead to infections or further delay in its healing. Perhaps such is the case when we feel emotional wounds. Some solitude can allow for some healing time.

In solitude, it does not have to be completely silent. We choose to listen to the music that we enjoy, for instance. We walk around listening to the birds chirp, some cars whizzing by, even seeing a good movie if we choose to. The point in solitude is to learn how to be comfortable with our own selves. This can only help us accept the painful circumstances that we have been experiencing or have experienced.

During our alone times, we can motivate ourselves to learn something new. There is so much to learn out there. Perhaps we can choose to learn to play the piano or guitar or drums. Maybe we can read a new book. We can make time for music appreciation of new music. We can learn to paint. Or cook a new recipe. We can learn to do carpentry, ride a horse, dance to hip-hop music. Be creative. With youtube, we now have access to world class teachers to learn something. You might just surprise yourself when you realize that you are inherently creative and capable of learning so much in this lifetime. Keeping our minds positively occupied is imperative in healing and rising.

Being in solitude also helps us be in touch with our own spirituality and contemplate how we rise up from disasters, losses and tragedies.

Gentle Reflective Questions

1. Where would be a good place for you to have some solitude?
2. Who would you want to talk to first to have some time for solitude?
3. When is the best time to have some sacred space or solitude after losses or tragedies?
4. What do you think solitude can help you with after having losses or tragedies?

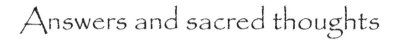

Answers and sacred thoughts

Phoenix Miracle Pearls

"If you love someone, you are always joined with them - in joy, in absence, in solitude, in strife."

~ Rumi

"There is a difference between loneliness and solitude. One will empty you and one will fill you".

~ Rumi

Gentle Exercises for the Spirit

1. Imagine taking a vacation by yourself. If a vacation is not possible, imagine taking off for a long weekend somewhere. It does not have to be far away. Perhaps we may want to visit a place where there is not as many people. We may even go an a retreat.

2. During our time of solitude albeit brief, we might want to take our laptops or computers or some notebooks to journal our thoughts. Let us do our best not to censor our thoughts. In other words, let us not judge the thoughts that we put into words. This is a way of being kind to ourselves. At times, after losses and tragedies, we become tough on ourselves or even blame ourselves for whatever happened. We get into a thinking mode of "if only I did this or if only I did that". By allowing ourselves to write freely during our solitude, we may end coming up with some profound perspectives and helpful in sights.

3. Others may want to bring their sketchbooks to do some drawings. We don't have to be artistic experts in drawing, painting, coloring or even creating collages. The idea is to be in touch and make friends with our

creativity while in solitude. Many times, we don't realize that we are creative.

Julia Cameron, in her book The Artist's Way wrote "While there is no quick fix for instant, pain-free creativity, creative recovery (or discovery) is a teachable, trackable spiritual process". In solitude, our creativity tends to blossom.

3. Get up. Stay present. Welcome the day. Gratitude.

Just to get up in the mornings is a gift we could be thankful for. Taking that first morning breath with mindfulness reminds us of the gift of life. Every moment that we breathe is beyond precious. A great habit to have is to choose to welcome the day and to stay present with each day we live.

When we get in touch with what we are thankful for, that is another day of living a life with joy.

When I think of gratitude, my mind goes back to my experiences doing short term medical missions in Africa. Most specifically, I recall the beautiful and joyful faces of the villagers in Mubende, Uganda. When our mission team first went to Uganda, we were welcomed with open arms by the villagers. The second time we went to visit there, our team was deluged with energizing welcome and with much gratitude. My Ugandan friends explained to me that it is one thing to go there and visit or do missions. But when we go back to visit for a second time, then that is the beginning of friendship. Remembering the grateful and happy faces of the villagers, especially the children, fills my heart much joy. I still vividly recall the singing and the dancing when the people of the town of Mubende welcomed us for the second time. Remembering their grateful faces, reminds me to be grateful.

The sheer grateful joy that I saw in the faces of the Mubende villagers will always be etched in my heart. It was quite amazing that in spite of the poverty and lack of resources in their village, the people remain so grateful and make time to sing and dance with us. The welcome they gave us was truly heartwarming and will never be forgotten.

In the Philippines, there is a concept called "utang na loob" (oo tang nah-lo-ob). It is a profound concept of gratitude literally meaning "a debt from inside or from within". It stems from a feeling of deep gratitude towards someone who has given or done a lot for us. The most important part of this concept, is that the grateful person never forgets this. There is almost a sense of loyal gratitude to the giver which then fuels the giver to give to others even more.

In addictions, one of the wise paradigms within the treatment process, is reminding people that "Gratitude is the Attitude".

A grateful person is truly a happy person. When we are grateful for the big and little things in our lives, we start feeling the blessings of what we have or not have. The happiest people I have known are usually the ones who are grateful regardless of the circumstances in their lives. When we pity ourselves for what we don't have or because we feel that our circumstances are hopeless, we start to forget about the healing power of gratitude.

When we are able to access the power of gratitude within us, regardless of our circumstances, our healing starts to solidify.

Gentle Reflective Questions

1. What do you feel grateful for?
2. Who have been examples of people you know who have grateful hearts?
3. When did you feel the most grateful in your life?
4. Where were you when you felt the most grateful?
5. Why do you think gratitude makes someone feel joy?

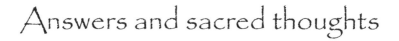

Answers and sacred thoughts

Phoenix Miracle Pearls

"Gratitude is not only the greatest of all virtues, but the parent of all others."

~ Cicero

"I would maintain that thanks are the highest form of thought, and gratitude is happiness doubled by wonder."

~ Gilbert K. Chesterton

Gentle Exercises for the Spirit

1. Think of the people you feel grateful for.
2. Send them thank you cards. Be specific as to what you are thanking them for.
3. Call someone to thank them about something good they had done for you.
4. Think of the people who are exemplars of gratitude.
5. Think of yourself and how you felt when you were thankful
6. Think of everything you feel grateful for. Write it all down.
7. Thank yourself for choosing to live your best life this very moment

4. Cherish moments with pockets of joy, beautiful sights and sounds.

When traumatic situations occur, we have to counter the painful pictures in our minds with more beautiful and gentler sights, sounds, actions, words and feelings. Within the waves of grief and despair, we can choose to allow ourselves some pockets of joy. Otherwise it is way too easy to slip into a full blown depression from a grieving state. That balance between grief and joy is important to maintain our sense of well-being.

Though grief has no time frame, it is important to stay grounded in the midst of it. It can be far too easy for us to stay in the abyss of feeling disconnected, wishing we still had our loved ones, and getting caught up with our despair.

One way to help us maintain a sense of connectedness to our lives is to focus on what brings us joy. If we mainly focus on the chaos of what we experienced, we will miss out on the beauty and joy that may surround us. For instance, I have waxed lyrical about the beauty of Nature, sunrises and sunsets. Communing with Nature has been a great healer for my soul.

What also helped me when I was feeling grief about my losses, was focusing on children's laughter as I watched them play. It also helped for me to listen to the sounds of smooth jazz every time I woke up every morning to soothe my spirit. The softer sounds can be an antidote to the painful sounds we may have experienced such as when someone yelled or screamed at us. Or if we heard loud sounds that brought us fear and discomfort in the past.

The pockets of joy that we may experience could be in the simplest things. For some, it is in choosing to savor the aroma of good coffee or tea. For me, I love smelling the scent of the ylang-ylang flower because it reminds me of the Philippines. So I put some ylang-ylang essential oils in a diffuser and that gives me a sense of olfactory comfort after I get home from work.

Some people love food and they resort to comfort foods when in grief but others don't have a taste for food. Many people love to eat chocolates which is a pocket of joy for them.

At work, instead of just white noise, I have a little gadget that emanates various nature sounds. I keep mine on ocean waves as this keeps me calm and meditative. That helps me stay very focused on what I am doing at work at the same time that it gives me simple joy just to hear the ocean waves.

Another pocket of joy for ladies I know is to go to a salon to get their manicure and pedicure. Having the time to do some self-care can be a joyful experience for some. Some men focus on fixing their cars or creating projects that give them joy. Recognizing the subtle joys that we get from such simple things, in between the waves of grief is healing in itself.

All our senses are affected when we experience disasters, losses and tragedies. The idea is to help heal the rawness of our senses by allowing ourselves to have some pockets of joy as salve for our emotional and sensory wounds.

Gentle Reflective Questions

1. What gives you joy?
2. Who are the people who give you joy?
3. When do you feel the most joy?
4. Where do you feel joy?
5. Why is feeling joy important in our healing?

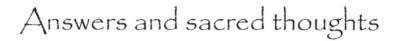

Answers and sacred thoughts

~ Phoenix Miracle Pearls~

"When you do things from your soul, you feel a river moving in you, a joy".

~Rumi

"The soul's joy lies in doing"

~ Percy Bysshe Shelley

Gentle Exercises for the Spirit

1. Let us remember when we felt joyful
2. We can go back to the time when we felt that joy
3. Imagine feeling those feelings of joy go through your mind, body and heart.
4. If it is difficult to remember, think about the people you know who exuded joy.
5. Remember their facial expressions, their actions, the way they interacted with you, what they said.
6. Think of something that made you feel joyful and carry it in your heart throughout the day. Keep practicing daily.

5. Commune with Nature.

There is nothing like waking up to a beautiful sunrise - that sacred and amazing ethereal break of dawn. To see all that colorful beauty, God's art work, in the sky is beyond imagination. I am fortunate to live in the heart of the beautiful Black Hills of South Dakota. The photographs I take don't do justice to the extraordinary nature I see out here.

Every morning, as I prepare for work, I could see the sunrise gently spreading across the skies from the side to the front of our home. Every sunrise I see is an original. The anticipation of seeing a new sunrise is something that restores my soul back to its delightful balance.

When I get back from work, I try to catch even a glimpse of incredible sunsets. There is also something special about watching the sun go down to give way for the moon to come out.

Communing with Nature is medicine for the soul. Nature, with all its plants and animals must have been made by the Creator to heal us.

Did you ever sit down under a tree and contemplate how amazing it is that trees ensure that we have our oxygen to breathe? Have you ever watched a cottonwood tree and see the sunlight go through its star-shaped leaves? Have you ever gardened and felt the healing power of watching plants grow and flowers bloom?

I will never forget my Linden tree. When I lived in Louisville, I had a very special Linden tree that I looked at every single day for many years from my bedroom window. At that time it was known to be the oldest Linden tree in Louisville and it was only supposed to have lived for 75 years.

Since I knew that the tree was close to that terminal age, I contacted a university that specialized in prolonging the lives of trees like this magnificent Linden tree. For many more years, I felt the comfort and healing power of that tree until it died. I had tears in my eyes when I realized it died yet I was grateful for the many years that it anchored my home and yard so beautifully. We truly are interconnected with everything.

I felt the same way about my two jade plants that I had nurtured for more than 25 years. Those exotic plants also died during my move from Louisville to the Pine Ridge reservation when I answered the Lakota tribal president's emergency call to help prevent youth suicides there.

And regarding animals, have you ever felt relief and comfort just cuddling up with your pet dog, cat or even being with horses?

There were very special experiences in my life that left an indelible mark in my mind. It was swimming with the dolphins, which I had done three times. One of those times was in Mexico and it was just after I lost a loved one. I was still feeling raw from the loss and was going through the motions of preparing my encounter with the dolphins. We were supposed to be in the position of the dead man's float when suddenly, with such impeccable grace and synchronicity, two dolphins put their noses steadfastly under the balls of my feet and lifted me up in the air with such amazing precision. While I was up in the air, I felt so incredibly exhilarated that during that time, I found my pocket of joy in the midst of my grief. After that experience, we had photos taken with one of the dolphins sweetly kissing my cheek. As I was walking out to the exit of the dolphin area, some tourist asked me, "What did you do? You look like you are glowing". I smiled to myself and marveled at the healing powers of dolphins and nature in general. Yes, I went back to work still feeling that magical glow from my dolphin encounter.

While taking a break during a tai-chi retreat in Estes Park, Colorado, I decided to ride a horse that day. The ground was blanketed with an inch of pure white snow. For some reason, the man in charge of the stables, insisted on me riding this enormous Belgian thoroughbred horse named Rudy. I initially thought that I would be riding a smaller thoroughbred. Though I was initially hesitant, I became more open to riding Rudy after he allowed me to lead him first. I softly whispered my fears to Rudy and how I hoped that he would be careful with me. As we went on a mountain trail, it was clear that Rudy was making sure that I did not get scraped by the bushes and tree branches on both sides of the trail. Rudy was very gentle and every now and then would look back as if to check on me as went on the trail to the top of a mountain clearing. Everything was going well and the mountain views were so spectacular that I couldn't help but feel overwhelmingly grateful for that experience. However, I did notice that Rudy's breathing was slightly labored as we went up the mountain. The altitude there was more than 10,000 feet. I reported this to the man in charge of the stables. He admitted that Rudy had some lung problems because of the altitude. I gave Rudy a hug and whispered thank you to him and hoped that his lungs got better.

After I got back home in the Black Hills, I kept thinking about Rudy. I even told Lawrence that I wish we could buy Rudy so he can live in a place with lesser altitude. Perhaps, his lungs would improve. This then compelled me to call the man who took care of Rudy to see if I could buy him. But no answer, even after I left messages.

A few months later, my cousin Jocelyn was needing a break so I recommended for her to go to Estes park for a tai-chi retreat. I also asked her to please check to see how Rudy was doing. When she got up there, she called me and sadly said that Rudy had passed away. I felt a painful pang of sadness. The spirit of this horse was so kind and gentle and for that brief time, we bonded. He helped me get over my fear of riding him because of his size. Rudy was there with me when I experienced the wondrous beauty of the mountain top scenery. I shall never forget Rudy. He is now in the heavens.

Communing with nature - with plants and animals - can truly help us heal and rise up because of that feeling of connectedness.

Gentle Reflective Questions

1. When was the last time you communed with nature?
2. Who were you with when you communed with nature or were you by yourself? What thoughts and feelings did you have being surrounded by nature?
3. Where did you go to be in touch with nature?
4. What was the most memorable experience for you when you were communing with nature?

Answers and sacred thoughts

Phoenix Miracle Pearls

"Nature itself is the best physician."

~ Hippocrates

"Love the world as your own self, then you can truly care for all things."

~ Lao Tzu

"We don't inherit the earth from our ancestors, we borrow it from our children."

~ Native American proverb

Gentle Exercises for the Spirit

1. Take a walk surrounded by nature. For example, there is a spiritual place in Lead, South Dakota called The Sanctuary. It is privately owned but open for free to the public. As we walk in there, there are windbreakers and umbrellas that people could borrow as needed. There are bronze statues with wise sayings from all over the world that we can contemplate on while walking in this beautiful meadow studded with birch trees on its edges. That area reportedly was where Chief Sitting Bull rested. There are seven horses that we can watch from the green meadow. We can always find a special place to commune with nature where it could stir our souls. Find your own sacred nature place.
2. Take notice of everything about nature as you walk on a trail.
3. Did you notice the plants? The trees and the flowers? What about some animals that may have crossed your path?
4. Take photographs if you wish or you can just enjoy what you see.

5. If you have pets, perhaps you can even bring them to your sacred place.

6. Discover your favorite animal. Do you dream about certain animals? Contemplate about the many characteristics of the animals you dream about. Are their traits similar to your traits?

7. Go to a lake, river or ocean. Enjoy the beautiful waters that grace our world. Think about how it would be without the clean waters of our world. Listen to the ocean waves.

8. Enjoy the sunrises and sunsets. Absorb the sacredness of the beautiful colors that grace our skies.

9. Find time with Nature wherever we may be.

6. Stay balanced. Proper sleep, nutrition and exercise. Think water. *Dance*

Our physical health is very important as many physical illnesses can actually affect our moods. Mindfulness in proper nutrition, sleeping soundly for approximately 6 to 8 hours and exercising are the essentials of staying healthy. When we are physically healthy, our brains function better and thus, our moods improve as well.

It is a good idea to get a wellness check with our Primary Care Provider. Prevention of illnesses is important and the collaboration between our Primary Care Provider is a significant aspect of our healing from our trauma.

Many people have experienced how stress and trauma had taken its toll on their bodies. For instance, I have three relatives who had been long-term care-givers to their spouses or other family members, and all three of them ended up having cancer. Was that a coincidence? I think not. Caregivers usually give of their time, energy and effort to loved ones or people who are ill. In the process of doing so, many times, they forget their own self-care because of their selfless big hearts.

Caregiving can be quite stressful as there is a sense of focus mainly on the one they are care-giving for, and not enough about themselves. Balance is not easy. It is imperative that people care for our care-givers. It would be helpful to relieve them episodically and give them time to just care for themselves. Respite places have been very helpful in situations where families have been caring for chronically ill loved ones.

Caregivers tend to absorb the ailments of their ill loved ones. There are many anecdotes and stories about caregivers ending up dying before the loved ones they had been caring for. Yes, caregivers need a lot of tender loving care as well.

Sleep is a necessary health habit that we all sometimes minimize. Lack of sleep can lead to problems with focus, attention span and concentration. It can also induce irritability, moodiness, depression, anxiety and agitation. Sleep deprivation can magnify our emotions - both negative or positive - and can interfere with the self-regulation of our emotions.

People tend to feel many of these symptoms when they are jet-lagging. I enjoy traveling everywhere in the world. However, jet-lag can be a real health hazard. It is a good idea to take a couple more days off before going back to work, if possible, after long-distance traveling from one side of the world to another.

It has been studied that at least 7 hours of sleep at night may protect telomeres from damage or may restore them on a nighttime basis. Telomeres are the caps at the end of chromosomes that protect our cells and genes. Longer telomeres are associated with less cellular aging. It has also been studied that the erosion of telomeres can be halted by reducing stress and can be stimulated to grow again.

We can lengthen and protect our telomeres by staying active, maintaining a healthy weight, limiting exposure to air pollution, meditation, eating healthy fats and vegetables.

Nutrition and wellness go hand in hand. We are what we eat. Many of us already know and perhaps even practice what mindfulness in nutrition is all about: consume less salt and sugars and more fruits, nuts and vegetables; drink plenty of water; eat regularly and control portion sizes; replace saturated fat with unsaturated fat; boil, steam, or bake foods rather than frying.

Presently there are many types of dieting. Some have to do with portions reduction, some focus on eating more proteins and less carbohydrates, some are proponents of intermittent fasting. It is always good to do some research and ask your Primary Care Provider what would be the best and most appropriate diet for you. For instance, when people have diabetes, hypertension, or heart disease, we may want our family physician to weigh in on what would be best for us. Getting a nutritionist consultation would also be helpful.

Exercising is vital for our health and wellness. It is well known that exercising helps raise our endorphins and serotonin levels and can be very helpful in keeping our moods stable. Antidepressants like the Selective Serotonin Re-uptake Inhibitors (SSRI) like Prozac (Fluoxetine), Zoloft (Sertraline), Paxil (Paroxetine), Celexa (Citalopram) and Lexapro (Escitalopram) work on leveling the serotonin in the brain. Exercising helps us control our weight, reduce our risks for heart disease, improve our mental health and moods, boosts our energy levels, help with our bone and muscle health, reduce our stress and tensions, helps our bodies manage blood sugar and insulin levels.

My favorite forms of exercising are dancing, yoga, tai-chi and walking.

During lunch breaks, I do my best to make time walking for 30 minutes, or doing yoga or tai-chi on my exercise carpet in my office. However, all my life, I've loved dancing. I inherited the love for dancing from my parents.

When I dance, I feel like my parents spirits are right there with me. Throughout my life, I've learned ballroom dancing, Flamenco dancing, modern jazz dancing, and many other ethnic dances. There is something about moving our bodies that stimulates our spirits, thus giving us a sense of freedom of expression. Dancing involves movements in all directions and is a total body-workout, which is why it has been said that it is the best exercise of all, besides that it is fun.

When I combine dancing, and do yoga and tai-chi to help stretch my muscles, along with meditation, things tend to be in balance for me. Nowadays we don't even have to go to dance classes. During this pandemic, having youtube to learn some dancercize moves or creating a playlist of our favorite dance songs that we can dance to, can be very helpful in maintaining our physical and emotional health. For those with physical disabilities and are unable to dance, they have chair-yoga and chair-dances. So, let us dance our hearts out as we are able to. Dancing freely to our internal rhythms can certainly help us de-stress and help loosen up our emotions. This can only help us let go of some of our pain from our losses and trauma.

Gentle Reflective Questions

1. Who is there for us to remind or coach us about our physical and mental well-being?
2. What kinds of exercises appeal to you and why?
3. Where do you go do your exercises?
4. When do you sleep the best? Do you dream?
5. Why do you think that nutrition is a big part of our well-being?

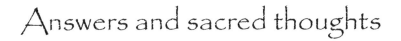

Answers and sacred thoughts

Phoenix Miracle Pearls

"Early to bed and early to rise makes a man healthy, wealthy and wise."

~ Benjamin Franklin

"Let food be thy medicine and medicine be thy food".

~ Hippocrates

Gentle Exercises for the Spirit

1. Monitor your sleep patterns. Learn how many hours you actually sleep. Turn down the shades and keep it dark at night. Be protective of your sleep and awake cycles.
2. Monitor your nutrition and eating habits. Do you eat when you are hungry or do you eat when your moods dictate it to you? Practice healthy and mindful eating. Seek the help of a nutritionist or your family physician.
3. Monitor your daily exercise. Do you have fun walking, dancing, doing yoga or tai-chi? What do you think would help motivate you to exercise?
4. Remind yourself daily: "I will take care of my body, mind and soul".

7. Go back to doing the things we love to do.

Go back to everything that used to make your heart smile. We may be ready to smile again. Sing, dance, play a musical instrument. Take walks in the park. Talk to a friend. Call people we have been meaning to call before. Write letters. Run. Ride a bike again. Fly a kite. Watch some romantic comedies. Watch old movies. Listen to our favorite songs and sing along with the radio while we are driving to work. Karaoke with family and friends. Travel if we can. Go to museums. Go bird-watching. Paint, draw, sculpt, write poems or stories, or just have long lingering thoughts and reflections about things we love. Be creative. Go where joy is, and let it find us. As a great Hindu sage once said, "Art is nearer to life than any fact can ever be." To which I would add this: Creative activity, gently pursued, helps our healing process flow.

There is usually a time after a tragedy, loss or disaster when one feels a sense of shock. There is an emotional paralysis. People feel as if something massive just ran over them. Healing times are different for everyone. Some people rise sooner than others. Don't pass judgment on ourselves or others; just step into the process and trust that results will eventually come.

Many surgeons now recommend that their patients begin walking around as soon as they are able. This is much better for the circulation in general. Normally, we have an inner knowing as to whether we can start walking around or not after a surgery. We know how much pain we feel. We can feel the physical healing happen as the pain gradually diminishes. We hesitantly attempt to rise up and start walking. Slowly at first, until we feel some bursts of pain again. And we stop a bit and rest. I believe that this is just as true for emotional and psychological pain as well.

Many times, it is far too easy to just want to remain isolated and in a cocoon for too long of a time after a tragedy or disaster happens. And to a certain degree this is understandable. The mind tries to protect us from getting hurt again. There is the fear factor: If we rise up, we might fall back again too quickly and feel the pain more than ever before.

It is wise to check in with ourselves. Just as with physical pain, we know when we start feeling less psychic hurt. I recall a time when tragedy struck our family, and that it was difficult for me to even answer phone calls from very dear childhood friends. I needed to consolidate my mind, and required a lot of reflective times. The world felt overwhelming. It was very compelling to recoil and just stay under the blankets in the comfort of my bed. My featherbed served as my all-too-comfortable cloud. Why would anyone want to leave that softness? Especially when the world seemed so harsh.

Knowing that I needed to start rising a bit, my siblings helped me by coming to my home and inviting me to do family activities, like going on a hay-ride in Huber Farms in southern Indiana. I recall that my senses were very acute at that time. Everything seemed almost too bright. The stimulation was almost deafening. But as I heard the children's laughter, as I saw the delight in their faces amidst the many pumpkins of all shapes and sizes, and I had a whiff of freshly-made apple cider and apple bread, something clicked inside of me. It was that blessedly familiar connection to the beauty and wonder of life.

After that outing, I slowly but surely started going back to the things I loved to do. I started to play my electric and acoustic guitars again. Music has always helped ease my mind so I did a lot of listening to music that soothed me. Smooth jazz. Oldies. Beatles' music. Chopin, Beethoven, Tchaikovsky. Returning to work was another big step. But once I decided to go, I easily settled down with my old routines and appreciated the support of my colleagues and co-workers. Most of all, I started to dance again.

Though we talk about going back to the things we loved to do, it is also good to keep learning new things as well. This was when I decided to learn to play the cello. This was also when I decided to belt out the song "Oh Darling" by the Beatles knowing that I may not ever be able to reach the high notes.

Before we know it, we can be back to our old world again. Our world before the tragedy happened. That world may not be completely the same anymore because that world has now evolved. That old world has now grown in spirit. We may still be a bit dazed from the tragic experience, but nevertheless we can experience being engaged and connected again with our loved ones and all the other people important to our lives. That is how it feels when we start rising. We start feeling grounded and connected again and that creates a platform for which we shall rise.

Gentle Reflective Questions

1. When did you start feeling like you could rise up again from your tragedy or loss?
2. How did you manage to go back to your old routines, to the world you had before the tragedy or loss?
3. Who was there for you, to help you rise up again?
4. Where and what part of your life did you begin to rise up after your heartbreak?
5. What did you learn about yourself as you were rising back up again from a tragic circumstance?

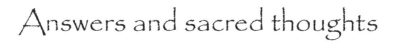

Answers and sacred thoughts

Phoenix Miracle Pearls

"Choose a job you love and you will never have to work a day in your life.".

~ Confucius

"Make the best use of what's in your power and take the rest as it happens."

~Epictetus

Gentle Exercises of the Spirit

1. Gentle thoughts:
   "I will go back to what I love to do."
   "I will rise up and embrace life."
2. Gentle words: Take a long deep breath, then exhale through your mouth very slowly. Whisper the above words to yourself three times.
3. Gentle actions: Think of something that you've wanted to do, something that is good for you and that you have been hesitant in doing. Invite a friend or family member to do this. In preparation for the event, and even during the event, repeat this healing phrase: "I will go back to what I love to do."
4. Now focus on what you really love to do and write them down. Then choose to do them.

8. Smile some more. Allow some lightheartedness. Humor.

There is nothing more beautiful than a heartfelt smile. When we feel forlorn or depressed, our facial expressions become more down-turned. Its as if we allow gravity just to take over our faces because we feel sad and hurt. Sometimes, the act of smiling can literally change the course of the day for people. It is like working from the outside in. The act of smiling triggers our brains to literally send us signals that change our moods for the better. It is like the 'faking it until we make it' concept.

This reminds me of an old song that was made famous by Nat King Cole that starts out with: "Smile, though your heart is aching..."

This song talks about the importance of smiling even though our hearts are breaking. In one aspect, it seems as though it tells us to repress our true feelings of pain from heartbreak. From another perspective, it tells us that by smiling, we can eventually overcome challenges and see life as something we can enjoy again. By smiling, we suppress our tearful feelings to allow us to cope with our day.

A smile from others can brighten up our day. Likewise, when we smile at others, we shine our light out to them. Heartfelt smiles are positive energies that can create a warm atmosphere among people.

We can see the effects of smiles when we are caring for babies. Babies tend to mimic their parents or guardians' facial expressions. They learn to associate something positive with their nurturers' smiles.

When we feel depressed, we can find it difficult to even smile. When we feel happy, our smiles are more upturned and our faces radiate more light. Smiles are very positively contagious. Have you ever tested this out?

Let us try going to work with a smile on our faces. When we smile at our co-workers we generate a chain reaction of smiles. We can observe this during staff meetings. Smiles from leaders in a work setting set a positive and friendly tone for the staff that words could not do as effectively.

On average, a smile uses 12 muscles and a frown, 11. Since humans actually tend to smile a lot, these muscles are stronger. Smiling activates that part of our brain that processes sensory rewards. So when we smile at someone they feel rewarded and vice-versa.

Smiling not only offers a mood boost but it also helps our bodies release cortisol, dopamine and endorphins that provide us with health benefits like lowered blood pressure, reduced stress, reduced pain and strengthened immune system.

A genuine smile is an open invitation that we are friendly and that we are wiling to interact with others. It can also mean that we are willing to cooperate and that we are worthy of another person's time and attention. This can only help us rise above our circumstances.

My heart's Smile

My heart's smile
begins and ends
with seeing you
May you feel my
laughter warm
your soul
May your day
be filled with
everything you wish
May your heart
be filled with
tenderness
May your life
be what you
desire
May your happiness
be for always
May your soul
be filled
with
immense love
beyond your
understanding
Now I see you
I see your heart
smiling too.

Gentle Reflective Questions

1. Who are the people in your life who have given you smiles?
2. What does it mean to you when someone smiles at you?
3. When do you usually smile? Give examples of when you smiled.
4. Why is it important for you to smile?
5. Where were the places that you remembered yourself smiling a lot?

Answers and sacred thoughts

Phoenix Miracle Pearls

"Silence and smile are two powerful words. Smile is the way to solve many problems and Silence is the way to avoid many problems."

~ Gautama Buddha

"Let my soul smile through my heart and my heart smile though my eyes, that I may scatter rich hearts."

~Paramahansa Yogananda

"Use your smile to change the world; don't let the world change your smile."

~ Chinese proverb

Gentle Exercises for the Spirit

1. Look in the mirror. Study your face. Then smile. Smile a little smile then a big smile. How do you feel when you smile?
2. Practice smiling at others. Smile at your family. Smile at your friends. Smile at your co-workers. Smile at your children and grandchildren.
3. Practice smiling when you hear music you like. Practice smiling to yourself when you think about something funny.
4. Practice wearing a smile as you walk, as you hike, as you dance, as you sing.
5. Practice smiling as you do your art, play your musical instruments, as you write, as you read.
6. Practice smiling until it becomes a positive habit.

9. Regress a bit. Learn to play again.

Some people find it silly just to regress and play. We all get caught up in being serious adults that we forget to nurture the child within us. Play is a vital part of life whether we are children or adults.

It has been said that Pablo Picasso, the great cubist artist, literally started learning how to paint like a child at age 64.

Psychiatrists and therapists may talk about "regression in the service of the ego". There are times when it is healing and healthy for us to just find the time to play like we did when we were children. When we regress, we start feeling the emotional freedom that we had as children. We stop judging ourselves and others. We start finding joy in the simplest things and the simplest actions.

When we allow ourselves to regress a bit, we give our selves permission to be light-hearted, silly, playful, curious, creative. When we experience losses and trauma, we become very serious. We hardly allow ourselves to play.

After my dad and my sister died within one year, natural grief made me feel so serious. So it was a breath of fresh air for me when my childhood friends from my elementary school called me to go to our reunion in San Diego. Initially, I was quite hesitant and told them I didn't think I would go. Then, I had a dream, about my sister and I playing in a meadow next to our home in the Philippines. We were catching dragonflies and would sit in the midst of tall grasses for hours just to watch those beautiful creatures fly around us. It felt like the dream was about my sister prompting me to go to my childhood reunion. Many of my elementary friends knew my sister. I woke up feeling refreshed and decided to go to the reunion. It was one of the best things I ever did.

I made reservations in our timeshare in Cabo San Lucas just to take a break. After regressing a bit and having so much fun with my childhood friends, I told them that I can accommodate seven other people in the timeshare and whoever wanted to come, then just join me there. Well, there were eight of us who went there and we enjoyed so much bonding with one another. Interestingly, we all found out that all eight of us lost loved ones within the last couple of years. There were no coincidences. The ones who ended up there were meant to be there together. It was quite healing for all of us to be there with others who have experienced the same loss and pain. We all played in our own way. We rode camels together by the beach. We sang all our old favorite songs and did karaoke. A few of us walked on the beach in the mornings. We watched beautiful sunrises and sunsets right from the terrace. We laughed at all our silly stories about ourselves. We shared all our childhood perspectives about one another. We just relaxed and played and allowed the sun to give us warmth and some tan.

I felt so rejuvenated and relaxed when I got back home. The beauty of some regression is that it allows us to heal, rise up and embrace our resilience. More so, our vacation together created a bonding of friends for a lifetime. We can never underestimate the significance of play as part of overcoming our trials and tribulations.

Gentle Reflective Questions

1. Who are the people you feel safe regressing with?
2. What would help you allow yourself to play and regress a bit?
3. Where can you see yourself enjoying a bit of regression?
4. When do you think you will have time to play?
5. Why is play important in our lives?

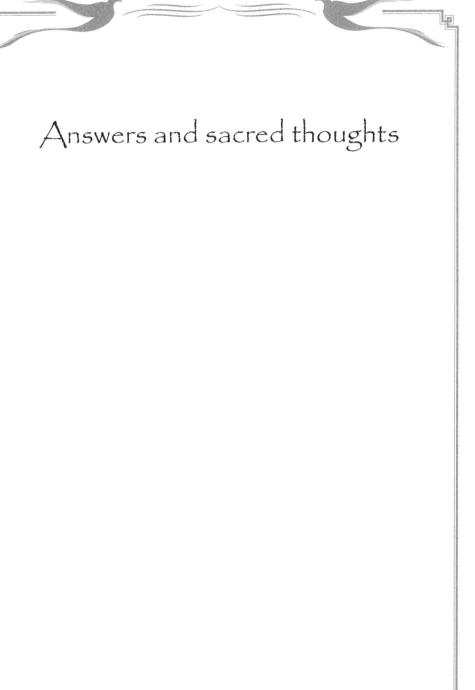

Answers and sacred thoughts

Phoenix Miracle Pearls

"A little nonsense now and then, is cherished by the wisest men"

~Anonymous

"The creation of something new is not accomplished by the intellect but by the play instinct."

~ Carl Jung

Gentle Exercises for the Spirit

1. Let us make time to just play
2. Allow ourselves to be child-like again
3. Observe the little children and the way they play
4. Find time to play with your children or grandchildren
5. Listen to what they say and be mindful of what they enjoy
6. Learn from our children
7. Go out and find a playground and just swing
8. Play some video games with your children or grandchildren
9. Play the old-fashioned board games
10. Follow a trail and playfully enjoy every step you take and what you see around you.
11. Invite family and friends to just go out and play together
12. Role play with your children or grandchildren just for fun
13. Play. Be creative.

10. Thank your critics and hug your supporters

There is much wisdom in the saying "what other people say about us is none of our business". No matter what we do in our lives, we will always have those who are our critics and those who are our supporters. People's opinions of us are based on their own experiences and realities that are not necessarily a reflection of us.

After going through losses and tragedies, at times it may be difficult to hear critical advice even from loved ones and friends. Many times, the critical comments, add to our frustration and irritation which end up making us isolate more. However, we can certainly learn from what people say, understanding that what they say are a product of what they have learned in their lives. What people say may not necessarily have anything to do with us at all. When it really gets better is when we actually thank the people who have been critical for sharing with us what they have gone through which we may or not use as lessons for us.

As we have critics, we also have supporters. Let us not take for granted the people who unconditionally uplift us. It is too easy to react to critics. In reality, the chief critic has always been ourselves anyway. Those who unwaveringly support us are true emotional anchors in our lives and help us rise up from our pain. They are like fuel to our healing.

Our unconditional supporters are our unsung winds underneath our wings. Let us thank them with love.

Gentle Reflective Questions

1. Who have been your critics? Your supporters?
2. When did you feel that you learned from a critic? When did you feel most supported?
3. Why is it important for us to have some critics and supporters?
4. Where were you when you felt supported most?
5. What was the most valuable critique that was given to you?

   What was the most valuable support ever given to you?

Answers and sacred thoughts

Phoenix Miracle Pearls

"It is one of the most beautiful compensations of this life that no man can sincerely try to help another without helping himself.".

~ Ralph Waldo Emerson

"It is a kingly act to assist the fallen."

~ Ovid

Gentle Exercises for the Spirit

1. Read a book about daily affirmations to start and end your day.
2. Practice unconditional affirmation of self and others.
3. Practice avoidance of criticisms towards self and others.
4. Practice finding the best in others and let them know.
5. Practice finding the best in our selves without judgment.
6. If for some reason, automatic critical thoughts occur, flip the switch and re-frame those thoughts to more positive and affirming ones.
7. Practice numbers 2,3, 4 and 5 daily.

11. Understand your fears

In my book The Courage to Encourage, I wrote that "Courage is born out of the greatest of fears. And courage is also gleaned out of the greatest of disasters and tragedies. To encourage our courage within is nothing less then divine". It is about acting or responding in spite of fears.

The coronavirus pandemic brought to light the courage and heroism of many front-liners in our healthcare profession. Many doctors and nurses have been exposed to, got infected with COVID-19 and many have died from dedicatedly serving and helping people who were ill. Despite great odds, our health care providers and hospital staff valiantly went to work even with the sad lack of Personal Protective Equipment (PPE) like masks, hospital gowns, gloves to protect them from getting infected themselves. They acknowledged their fears yet they chose to have the courage to respond and sacrifice themselves for the welfare and well-being of others. Not only did they bravely go to work each day to muster up courage and overcome their own fears, they made a solid decision to give their lives for others if they have to. No greater love do we know than to give of our lives if we have to for others.

When we understand our fears, we can choose to overcome them and rise above them.

Facing our fears is one of the biggest hurdles we work on to rise above circumstances. As we are able to face our fears, we then begin to understand that being courageous does not mean that we don't get fearful.

For instance, if we are being bullied and when we finally are able to stand up to bullies, we realize that we are courageous after all. Interestingly, bullies tend to feed off their victims' fear of them. Once the bullies see that the ones being bullied are not afraid of them anymore, their sense of false bully-power is not so powerful anymore.

Understanding and facing our fears allow us to grow and help us rise up to life's many challenges. Many people whose fears tend to rule their lives may benefit from therapy or counseling.

Gentle Reflective Questions

1. Who has ever caused you fear in your life?
2. What were you feeling when you were facing your fears?
3. Where were you when you felt quite fearful?
4. Why is it important to face our fears?
5. When did you feel the most fearful? And when did you feel the most courageous?

Answers and sacred thoughts

Phoenix Miracle Pearls

"Being deeply loved by someone gives you strength, while loving someone deeply gives you courage"

~ Lao Tzu

"Nothing in life is to be feared, it is only to be understood. Now is the time to understand more, so we may fear less."

~ Marie Curie

Gentle Exercises for the Spirit

1. Gentle thoughts: "I will overcome my fears"
   "I am braver than I think".
2. Gentle actions: "I will write about what I fear; and I will overcome it"
3. If fears tend to overwhelm us and affect many parts of our lives:
   Seek therapy to learn to overcome fears.

12. Reframe your thoughts positively

Many times, negative thoughts enter our minds automatically. Many people with depression and anxiety battle these thoughts daily. Cognitive Behavioral Therapy (CBT) has been an effective therapeutic tool that Aaron Beck MD jumpstarted to help people reframe their thoughts towards the positive. The automatic negative thoughts many times end up being a habit. Like any negative habits, they can be broken and redirected towards more positive habits.

"Cogito, ergo sum". Descartes stated that "I think, therefore I am". He found that he could not doubt that he existed because he was the one doing the doubting in the first place. With our thoughts, we eventually create our own realities. These realities affect our temperaments, our attitudes and our choices in our lives. Our thoughts are powerful energies of our minds.

If the automatic negative thoughts persist and interrupt our daily functioning, it may be best to seek some help with therapy and to learn the healing effects of Cognitive Behavioral Therapy.

There are ten cognitive distortions identified in Cognitive Behavioral Therapy:

- All or nothing thinking: This involves seeing things in absolute extremes; in black or white.

- Mental filter: When one takes a small event and focuses on it exclusively, filtering out anything else.
- Overgeneralization: This is when someone makes a rule about a single event or a series of coincidences. People usually use the word "never" or "always" in their sentences.
- Discounting the positive: This is a cognitive distortion that involves devaluing or ignoring good experiences that have happened to you.
- Jumping to conclusions: This involves "mind-reading" or thinking that others are going to react in a certain way and "fortune-telling" or predicting events will unfold in a certain way to avoid something difficult.
- Magnification: this is when people exaggerate the importance of shortcomings and problems while minimizing the importance of desirable qualities.
- Emotional reasoning: this is when you judge yourself or your circumstances based on your emotions. When you use emotional reasoning to conclude that you are a worthless person, this can lead to self-defeating behaviors.
- Labeling: this involves making a judgment about yourself or someone else as a person. When people label themselves as "bad" then they tend to end up believing that it would be hard for them to be "good".
- Should statements: "Should" statements are about feeling short of what we think we could truly attain. Thus this leads to feelings of being a failure.
- Personalization and blame: when you blame yourself or others for circumstances that essentially were out of your control. An example is when people blame themselves for a childhood abuse and think that they were to blame for it.

Cognitive Behavioral therapy helps us challenge and identify these cognitive distortions and replace them with more objective and realistic thoughts. It also involves using strategies to help overcome the automatic negative thoughts by journaling, role-playing, mental distractions.

Being aware of our cognitive distortions can help us "flip the switch" from a negative to a more positive mind-frame. This takes practice and can be very helpful in our healing from tragedies and losses.

Gentle Reflective Questions

1. Who do you tend to blame for things that are happening in your life?
2. What cognitive distortions have you utilized?
3. When did you find yourself using these cognitive distortions?
4. Why do you think you used these cognitive distortions?
5. Where did you remember observing some of these cognitive distortions in others and in yourself?

Answers and sacred thoughts

Phoenix Miracle Pearls

"We are shaped by our thoughts; we become what we think. When the mind is pure, joy follows like a shadow that never leaves."

~ Gautama Buddha

"There is nothing either good or bad but thinking makes it so".

~ William Shakespeare

Gentle Exercises for the Spirit

1. Identify your cognitive distortions
2. Identify your positive thoughts and reactions
3. Practice positive thinking
4. Practice positive actions
5. Reward yourself for positive thoughts and actions
6. Practice having a positive attitude daily

13. Discover beauty in everything

Have you ever just gotten up early in the morning to watch your children or grandchildren's beautiful faces while they are still sleeping? Did you ever wake up early to watch the colorful morning sunrise unfold before your eyes? Have you ever stopped just to absorb the beauty of nature like listening to birds and contemplating the various shapes of the clouds in the sky? If you do not live around nature, have you ever taken some time just to commune with nature? There is beauty everywhere. God's art work is everywhere around us. We are surrounded by beauty yet at times we take things for granted and do not see.

We might ask, how can we see beauty if we are still reeling from disasters, losses or tragedies in our lives? One thing is focusing on what is beautiful and joyful. Another thing is discovering beauty in what we may have taken for granted while we were busy healing.

Have you ever paid attention enough to discover the beauty of the hearts of the people you know? Were you able to discover the beauty in others who in the past you may have judged because of their actions? Do you think it is possible to find beauty in the most horrific experiences like disasters, for instance?

Beauty is truly in the eyes of the beholder. What may be beautiful to us may not necessarily be seen as beautiful by others. When we see beauty in others, we see beauty in ourselves. We tend to project ourselves on others. Being mindful in seeing the beauty in others allows us to see our own beauty within.

It is healing to discover beauty in everything. For instance, people might ask about what beauty can we see in a pandemic. Without denying the pain of people directly affected by losses and trauma during the pandemic, we also saw the beauty in the hearts of our front-liners risking their lives to save others. We saw the beauty in the souls of people who made sure that their families were protected from the virus by following public health guidelines. We saw the beauty in the compassion of many people towards each other when they made sure that people had enough food. We saw the beauty of the people in Spain and Italy through social media when they played music in the balconies for one another. We saw the beauty in families when they actually found time to have dinner with each other.

In the midst of what seems to be darkness, we can find beauty in knowing that the light will ultimately shine though our hearts in tackling this pandemic together as a world.

> "To walk in beauty is perhaps to see everyone and our world through the eyes of our Creator."

> ~ author

Gentle Reflective Questions

1. Who do you think are beautiful and why?
2. Why do you think discovering beauty is important in our healing?
3. When did you feel the beauty of certain situations circumstances?
4. Where do you see beauty that you never forgot?
5. What do you feel is the most beautiful thing you have experienced in your life?

Answers and sacred thoughts

Phoenix Miracle Pearls

"Never lose an opportunity of seeing anything beautiful, for beauty is God's handwriting".

~ Ralph Waldo Emerson

"Everything in the universe is a pitcher brimming with wisdom and beauty."

~ Rumi

"The only lasting beauty is the beauty of the heart".

~ Rumi

Gentle Exercises for the Spirit

1. Close your eyes and think of someone, something, a situation that is beautiful to you
2. Think about why people are beautiful to you.
3. Think about why something or situations are beautiful to you.
4. Think of the last time that you saw something or someone as beautiful.
5. Think of when someone thought you were beautiful
6. Think of when you thought you were beautiful
7. Discover the beauty all around you. What do you see?

14. Learn to set healthy limits and boundaries.

Setting healthy limits and boundaries allows us to focus on ourselves while we are healing and rising up from situations of losses and tragedies. Many times, as much as we love our families and friends, we have to let them know that we are in the midst of healing and need some healthy time to help ourselves. Being truthful and honest helps with establishing healthy boundaries.

At times, our own loved ones may feel rejected or even get angry when we establish some limits. Eventually you will be able to explain the necessity of setting healthy limits and boundaries to them as you are able to. Those who love us will love us anyway, and will respect our desire to heal. Some may not understand this but it is important that we set boundaries so we can focus on our own healing. Without healthy boundaries, it is more difficult to focus on our own self-care because it is too easy to be dragged into other people's problems. It will be hard to help others if we don't know how to help ourselves first. The idea is not unlike putting the oxygen on ourselves first before putting the oxygen on another when we are in an airplane. That makes it clear that if we are not okay, we will not be able to help others the way we would like to.

At times, people will borrow money or things from us repetitively.

They make promises about paying the debt when they

supposedly have money or get their next paycheck. Usually there is an urgency for the reason that they are borrowing money from us. Then, they feel entitled to borrow more money even though they have not paid for the funds that they promised to pay for. Sadly, they start getting upset because we decide to set limits and boundaries and let them know that we will not dole out money anymore because they have broken their promise of paying for their debt. Not paying a debt is a form of disrespect.

As much as we want to be generous and giving, we also need to take care that we don't enable others to use us nor take us for granted. On top of this, they feel offended when we don't give them anymore hand-outs and put us down for not "giving". Setting healthy boundaries is healthy not only for us but also for the people who tend to take advantage of our giving nature. It is best if we help people to earn for what they need by giving them jobs, and to help people be self-sufficient. In dealing with family or friends who are addicted to drugs or alcohol or gambling, it is much better to just buy them food or make sure they have shelter, or refer them for help. Giving them cash would just lead them to buy their alcohol or drugs that could potentially hurt or kill them.

There are also instances when people tend to take up a lot of our time emotionally. They call us only when they have problems or when they need something. They don't seem to even ask us how we are and they proceed to then barrage us with their problems. They repeat this over and over as we allow them to. Perhaps these are the people who may benefit from therapy. Setting healthy boundaries will help us heal ourselves from our own losses and trauma because we can then focus more on ourselves to do the work we need to heal and rise up.

Gentle Reflective Questions

1. Who do you feel you may have difficulties setting limits and boundaries with?
2. What benefits do you see in setting healthy limits and boundaries?
3. Where do you think would be the best place to talk to family or friends regarding setting limits and healthy boundaries?
4. Why do you think it had been difficult to set these healthy limits?
5. When do you think is the best time to establish healthy boundaries with others?

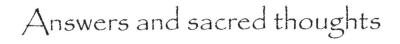

Answers and sacred thoughts

Phoenix Miracle Pearls

"I am not what happened to me. I am what I chose to become."

~ Carl Jung

"You are what you do, not what you say you'll do."

~ Carl Jung

Gentle Exercises for the Spirit

1. Think about times when looking back you knew you needed to set healthy limits and boundaries.
2. Think about times when you thought that you may have been enabling others.
3. Practice setting boundaries by talking to your loved ones about your need to focus on yourself as you are healing and rising up. You might want to write down what you want to say to them before you speak with them if this makes you feel more comfortable.
4. Be prepared for your loved ones reactions. Some may understand and some won't. How would you handle those situations?
5. Feel the freedom in setting healthy boundaries.

15. Forgive. Wish our spirits to soar

Forgiveness is not an easy endeavor when we feel hurt. It is a gift we need to decide to give ourselves. Not forgiving is a heavy weight on our spirits. We can decide to forgive the person though not necessarily their destructive actions. Some people are easy to anger yet forgive easily. Some feel so hurt by whatever circumstances hurt them that it takes them a much longer time to forgive. Many times we are unable to forgive because of our false pride as well. In reality, many work on the process of forgiving themselves for not forgiving. The truth is that it hurts more deeply not to forgive.

Carrying anger and resentments affects us physically, emotionally and spiritually. Resentments are like emotional cancers that pervade our beings. They literally eat us up and consume us. Anger makes our blood vessels constrict to the point of damaging our heart and other target organs of our body. Because we are human, anger is within norm. However when anger escalates into rage is when we need to think twice before unnecessary regrettable emotional explosions occur.

Holding on to hurt feelings and emotional pain can leave us feeling depressed, anxious and moody. It can destroy relationships with family, friends and loved ones. The internal work of letting go of our inner pain is a vital process of first forgiving ourselves for allowing others to hurt us so much. People may say, "Why should I be the one to forgive when they were the ones who hurt me?" Forgiveness does not mean unwittingly or wittingly subjecting ourselves to the same actions of others that hurt us.

However, there is a big difference between forgiveness and enabling. Forgiveness does not mean that we continue to give a loved one with addiction more alcohol because we forgave them for their behaviors. People who enable may do so accidentally by giving people money, for instance, when they don't know that a person is addicted and using the money given to them for their addictions. Forgiveness may require healthy boundary-setting as well.

G. K. Chesterton wrote:

> *"To love means loving the unlovable;*
> *To **forgive** means pardoning the unforgivable;*
> *Faith means believing the unbelievable.*
> *Hope means hoping when everything seems hopeless."*

This is a beautiful spiritual quote though I would have to add that forgiveness refers to pardoning the person, but not the destructive actions.

We can always forgive and love the person, though not their unlovable actions.

Forgiveness is incredibly significant in healing our spirits. When we let go of all the resentments, we feel a lightness within our beings that lessens the internal pressures within us. To forgive is not only to help heal others but to heal ourselves from the emotional wounds that hurt us in the past. We need that unconditional divine lightness of being to be able to soar above our losses and tragedies.

Gentle Reflective Questions

1. Who do you feel you need to forgive? Who do you need to ask for forgiveness? Do you feel you need to forgive yourself?
2. What is the importance of being able to forgive to you?
3. Where do you think you could visualize yourself forgiving someone?
4. Why do you think you need to ask for forgiveness?
5. When do you think is the best time to forgive and/or ask for forgiveness?

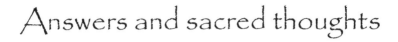

Answers and sacred thoughts

Phoenix Miracle Pearls

"Good to forgive, best to forget."

~ Robert Browning

"Let us forgive each other - only then will we live in peace".

~ Leo Tolstoy

"To err is human, to forgive, divine."

~ Alexander Pope

Gentle Exercises for the Spirit

1. Let us think of the people we may have hurt. Have we apologized to them? Perhaps we can make a list.
2. Let us think of the people who have hurt us. Some of them may have passed away already and some may have moved far away. Some still live around us. Write a letter asking for forgiveness to those we have hurt. Write a letter to people who have hurt us and tell them that we do forgive them. We can keep these letters and not send them to those people. Eventually, we may even be able to make time to do a ritual or personal ceremony. Some read their letters for those who have passed away and burn those letters safely and let the smoke pass up to the skies. Some send apology letters to people who are still around.
3. Let us write a letter to ourselves. A letter of apology to ourselves and also of self-forgiveness for allowing ourselves to be in situations that required forgiveness to heal.

WE SOAR

1. Embrace our faith even more

Faith has always given us a reason to hope when things are down. When we feel that there is no other way out of whatever it is that made us feel a rock-bottom situation, it allows us to choose to look up. Only then do we slowly realize that the rock-bottom situation was merely a platform to catapult ourselves to soar towards the Light.

Faith is different for everyone. Some people may find answers to their existential questions with their religion. Some may feel hope with their spirituality. Those who don't look to a Higher Source may find their faith from within. Some choose not to have faith at all and hang on to a state of disbelief about their circumstances.

Embracing our faith is like embracing hope for ourselves. To believe is to understand deeply that there is a power greater than our selves that is the source for everything that is happening to us. There is a general sense of profound hope when we believe in a source greater than us.

To doctors and scientists, spontaneous remissions or healing are difficult to explain. Religious and spiritual people use the word "miracles" when people have spontaneous recoveries and healing that can not be fully explained by our physicians. Besides faith, some people have perspectives that see life as positive and hopeful whereas others my see the gloominess and darkness of life. The spirit, mind and body can impact a person's healing. When we add faith and the desire to heal on a deep level, perhaps these can help create the healing "miracles" that we can not seem to explain scientifically.

Hope is also born out of faith. To hope is to imbue within us the utmost positivity for a desired outcome in our healing. To have faith is to believe without doubt that we will soar beyond our difficulties.

Gentle Reflective Questions

1. Who do you know has experienced spontaneous remission? Or have you read about spontaneous healing and remissions?
2. What do you think faith does to people who are healing from losses, illnesses, and trauma?
3. When do you think spontaneous healing tend to happen?
4. Why do you think faith is important in rising up from losses, trauma or tragedies?
5. Where have you known about healing that was hard to explain?

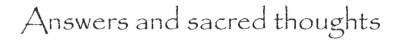

Answers and sacred thoughts

Phoenix Miracle Pearls

"Faith is being sure of what we hope for, and certain of what we do not see."

~ Hebrew 11:1 St. James bible

"Faith is to believe what you do not see; the reward of this faith is to see what you believe."

~ St. Augustine

"To one who has faith, no explanation is necessary. To one without faith, no explanation is possible."

~ Thomas Aquinas

Gentle Exercises for the Spirit

1. Let us contemplate on our faith. Who or what do we believe in?
2. Let us think about people who have been healed when their illnesses seemed desperate.
3. Let us remember who have recovered in a "miraculous way" and the doctors could not explain why.
4. Let us understand the connection between mind, body and spirit and faith.
5. If we know someone who had a spontaneous remission from a terminal illness, get to know them and talk to them. Ask them what they believed helped heal them.
6. Think about how faith can help heal ourselves to rise above our losses and tragedies.

2. Practice compassion and kindness especially when it feels hard to do.

It is very difficult to practice compassion and kindness when we are depressed and angry about our losses and tragedies. But it can be done if only we choose to. When we feel depressed or in grief, we may end up feeling a sense of "emptiness" whereby we feel that we are unable to give or feel love.

One of my patients insightfully shared with me that when she was not on her medications, she did not feel the love of her family nor did she feel love for them. Once she was back on her medications, she felt more balanced and back to herself. She intimated that she was able to feel her love for her family as well as feel their love for her again. Though her situation was based more on paranoid symptoms, when one is feeling depressed from losses or tragedies, the feelings of connectedness dissipate.

Thus, it becomes hard to practice compassion or even kindness towards others because of that feeling of disconnection. To be able to choose to give compassion and kindness again, we need to be able to do some reality checks. We can choose to look at our history and know that our family had loved us all along. However, when we continue to feel that sense of protracted emptiness whereby it starts to affect out relationships with our loved ones, that would be a good time to ask for professional help.

There are times when grief can slide into depression that would require therapeutic help. When our feelings of disconnection with our loved ones start to detrimentally affect many facets of our lives, then it is important to be able to ask for help. Otherwise our families may need to do some interventions so we can get the help we need. The interventions could be the most compassionate act that families could do to help their loved one who is struggling with mental health problems like complicated depression, anxiety, severe mood swings, psychosis, Post-traumatic Stress Disorder or Substance Use problems.

Gentle Reflective Questions

1. Who are the people who have shown you kindness and compassion?
2. What situations did you feel that others have shown you kindness and that you have shown others kindness?
3. Where did you feel that others were kind to you?
4. Why do you think that compassionate and kindness are necessary to heal and rise up?
5. When did you give kindness and compassion to others?

Answers and sacred thoughts

Phoenix Miracle Pearls

"Compassion is love's passion."

~ author

"Kindness in words creates confidence. Kindness in thinking creates profoundness. Kindness in giving creates love.

~ Lao Tzu

Gentle Exercises for the Spirit

1. Remember who have been compassionate and kind to you and what they did.
2. Do a random act of kindness no matter how big or small.
3. Think about ways to show our kindness and compassion to others.
4. Think of ways to be kind to ourselves.
5. Practice compassion and kindness daily.

3. Learn to laugh at ourselves. Laugh heartily, Laugh tenderly.

Being able to laugh at ourselves is true progress. There is something about not taking ourselves so seriously that can be so healing. As we grow up, we oftentimes become too serious and forget to laugh and be a bit easier on ourselves. Lightheartedness balances out the heavy situations in our lives. Once we realize that we can laugh about whatever we went through, then we begin to realize that we are actually healing, rising and soaring from a painful situation. It is very difficult to laugh or be lighthearted when we have gone through trauma or tragedies in our lives especially when our losses or trauma have been recent or acute.

My sister Marissa, my cousin Jocelyn, my high school friend Gina and my elementary school friend Daisy are excellent examples of people who can make anyone laugh at our own humanity. Their sense of humor and wicked wit can make one irreverently laugh at the most serious situations. They are the best teachers at learning to laugh at ourselves.

Laughter is truly the best medicine. Even as a child, I recalled this concept from reading Readers' Digest and laughing at its simple jokes.

I also remember feeling shocked to see one of my supervisors telling jokes in a comedy club when I was a psychiatric resident. When I spoke with him about it, he told me how healing and therapeutic it was for him to make people laugh. Blessed are the people who eventually see some humor in the toughest situations.

In 1995, a family physician from Mumbai, India did research on laughter being the best medicine. He then started a "laughter club" in his community. His wife was a hatha yoga practitioner and eventually the laughter club evolved into "laughter yoga". The belief was that prolonged voluntary laughter provides the same physical and mental benefits as spontaneous laughter without the need for jokes or humor. Then participants start to laugh without reason until the laughing becomes real.

Laughter provides the body with a cardio-work-out. They say that 10 minutes of laughter provides the same benefits as 30 minutes spent on a rowing machine. Laughter can also reduce blood pressure, increased antibodies that protect the bodies from viruses, bacteria and other infections. It can improve the immune system. Laughter is a great medicine to help us soar from our pain.

Gentle Reflective Questions

1. Who in your life makes you laugh?
2. What makes other people funny? What makes you funny?
3. When was the last time you laughed your heart out?
4. Where did you remember laughing so hard?
5. Why do you think laughter is very important to our healing and soaring above our trials and tribulations?

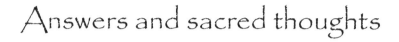

Answers and sacred thoughts

Phoenix Miracle Pearls

"Against the assault of laughter, nothing can stand."

~ Mark Twain

"The art of medicine consists of amusing the patient while nature cures the disease".

~ Voltaire

"Laughter is the sun that drives winter from the human face."

~ Victor Hugo

Gentle Exercises for the Spirit

1. Find time to watch a comedy. Let us understand what we are laughing about. Some people find certain things funny while others are unable to laugh about certain situations. Explore within as to what made something so funny to us that made us burst out in laughter.
2. Find time to be with people who make you laugh. The best laughter is not necessarily triggered by jokes, but by the positive contagion of someone who is laughing about something. Watch how contagious laughter can be.
3. Let us think about something that makes us laugh at ourselves.
4. Remember a situation that seemed serious to us in the past and now looking back, that situation makes us laugh.

4. Consider every moment a gift.

In life, we make choices about our experiences and our well-being. When we choose to be mindful of every second that we live, life starts to have more meaning and purpose. If we choose to take our lives for granted, we then go into a spiral of neglect and before we know it, we miss the best things in our lives. When we choose to see each moment as a gift, we start to value life and we start to be cognizant of our life purpose.

Basic happiness seems to be genuinely linked to being thankful for everything in our lives. When we choose to see every second of our lives as a gift, this teaches us to be even more grateful and consequently be more content and happy with ourselves and our circumstances. Making the most of our present teaches us to enjoy every second of our lives until it becomes a joyful chain of moments.

Children are the best in teaching us about living in the present. When children ages 3 to 5 play, they are very focused on the present and what they are playing with. They don't worry about the past nor the future because they are completely immersed in their moment. People who worry too much about the future tend to be anxious and those who tend to ruminate about the past tend to be depressed. Appreciating every moment we live, we begin to understand the importance of our lives. It allows us to learn to be thankful about our lives and to delight in each moment.

While meditating up in Machu Picchu in Peru, the

incredible environment there emphasized to me the beauty of the gift of life. While looking at the ruins, I came to appreciate the wisdom of the Incas and the lives they may have lived during those ancient times. What we do today impacts our future generations as what the Incas did then has impacted our generation. They taught us that building a stone fort on a mountain top that seemed impossible, was possible. This gift of life allows us to believe in all the possibilities that life can offer. By treasuring our lives as gifts, we can pass on to others the vitality of the lives we live.

When we pay special attention to the here and now, and that life is a present we give ourselves and others, this tends to help us soar above trauma and tragedies. We strengthen our minds to value each moment which can help soften the harshness of the past and anxieties about the future.

Gentle Reflective Questions

1. Who do you know sees their life's moments as gifts?
2. When do you feel thankful about moments in your life?
3. Where do you feel you appreciate the moments of your life?
4. Why do you think it is important to treat each moment of your life as a present?
5. What do you consider is the most important moment of your life?

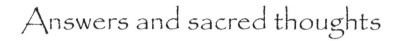

Answers and sacred thoughts

Phoenix Miracle Pearls

"Live in the present, launch yourself on every wave, find eternity in each moment.".

~ Henry David Thoreau

"At some point you just have to let go of what you thought should happen and live in what is happening."

~Anonymous

Gentle Exercises for the Spirit

1. Let us concentrate just on the moment. The now.
2. Let us focus on just drinking our glass of water, slowly, evenly and gradually. Feel how the water enters our mouths and down our esophagus and into our stomach. Savor that. Let us feel grateful that we are alive enough to feel refreshed by water.
3. Have a conversation with a family member or a friend. Look at who you are conversing with. Observe how our loved one talks. Observe their facial expressions and body language. Enjoy the best in the person you are conversing with. Remember that this person is a gift in your life. Appreciate the sound of their voice, the sparkle in their eyes, their hand gestures as they talk.

5. Find perfection in people's imperfections. Apologize.

When we love someone, what may be seen as imperfections by others, seem perfect to us through our love for that person. When our hearts are filled with love, we generally see our loved ones' quirks and awkward actions as lovable. What others may see as weird, may well be delightful to us because we love someone. It does not mean that we see the perfection in the imperfections all the time. For if we have arguments with our loved ones, what we previously saw as sweet and perfect become annoying and frustrating imperfections. Many times, we forget that we are only human and subject to changes of moods, perceptions and ideas.

When our children were still babies, they seemed just perfect to us. I know of loving parents who saw their babies as perfect in spite of having been born with physical defects. Babies seem perfect to us because we have this inherent spiritual feeling that a baby is life's longing to extend beyond ourselves. Seeing our babies as perfect may have to do with their lovable innocence. We see their spirits as a clean slate - a tabula rasa. As we all grow up, we end up loading our lives with many defenses that shield us from our innate innocence.

To find perfection in people's imperfections does not mean that we enable their inappropriate, negative or destructive actions. It simply means that behind all the masks of defenses and unlovable actions lies the pure innocence of a human being created by our highest source.

The beauty in finding the best in people is we then discover the best in ourselves as well. When we begin to see the innocence in others, we start to see the innocence in ourselves. This can only help us soar above the reactivity that we may have felt about people as we were in the initial phase of healing from losses and tragedies.

When going through losses or tragedies, our grief may make us feel that our lives are so imperfect. We tend to see darkness far easier than we see light. We may even question what seems to be the overt imperfection of God's plan. We hardly even see the people who we love because grief gets in the way of seeing our loved ones' perfect hearts. Feeling disconnected may make us feel detached and in limbo. We may even feel that the people who love us are so imperfect that they would not understand what we are really feeling inside.

Because we understand that we are human, and thus we may wittingly or unwittingly hurt others, it is healing for us and others when we apologize if we hurt others. There is much love and acceptance when we apologize from our hearts. A genuine apology can heal hurts and resentments that can lead to better relationships with others. There is perfection in that.

As we start rising from the depths of despair and grief, we start seeing the light again. We start feeling connected again. This is when we take a look back to where we were to get a true perspective of how losses may have affected us. We start seeing life's divine synchronicity and perfection once again. We start realizing that people who love us are there for us. And from a spiritual standpoint, that is just perfect in spite of what we think about their personalities. For love makes perfect all of our imperfections when we realize that we are exactly who we need to be. And others are exactly who they need to be. With love, there is no judgment of others nor ourself. With love, we see the perfection of drawing strength from within to soar up beyond our trials to hopefully give light to others.

Gentle Reflective Questions

1. Who are the people you know whose imperfections are perfect for you?
2. When did you feel that someone's imperfections became perfect?
3. What was a going through your mind when you were thinking about someone who you saw was perfect because of their imperfection?
4. Why is it important to see the perfection in someone's imperfection?
5. Where did you meet someone who you felt was a perfectly imperfect person? Do you see yourself as a perfectly imperfect person or someone who is imperfectly perfect?

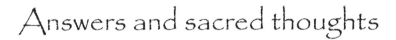

Answers and sacred thoughts

Phoenix Miracle Pearls

"To be perfect is to develop expanding imperfection."

~Ethylios

"It belongs to the imperfection of everything human that man can only attain its desire by passing through its opposite."

~ Soren Kierkegaard

Gentle Exercises for the Spirit

1. Let us look deep within us and discover what are our imperfectly perfect traits are.
2. Then, let us look at others and discover perfectly imperfect, lovable traits that they have.
3. When you fell in love with someone, do your best to remember imperfectly perfect traits and behaviors that you remembered observing in them.
4. Remember when you saw someone's imperfections as perfect and when did this turn back to imperfections

6. Open up to rainbows and delight in every color

Celebrating and enjoying the differences in people can at times be challenging. There is comfort in the familiar and similarities with people. When we were young, we were mainly exposed to family and people who "were like us". As we grew up, learned more, traveled more and expanded our ability to understand different kinds of people more, we then see the beautiful rainbow colors of people in our world.

My children grew up with a mixture of many cultures and ancestry running through their veins. They are a combination of Filipino, Spanish, German, English and Chinese. When I did my Ancestry DNA test, the results came out with a big percentage of my heritage coming from the Southeast Asian and the Polynesian Islands. Many times, when I ask my patients what their ancestry or culture is, they would answer, "White" or "Brown" or "Black". I would usually respond to them that "Those are colors. I mean your cultures. For example, if you are white, did your ancestors come from England, Germany, Sweden or the Netherlands?" Then they all understand, and they start talking about being "Heinz 57" or being "a mutt" or mixtures of various races and cultures.

When we feel comfortable with our our own color and race and that of others, it helps us be less judgmental of ourselves and others. When we are judgmental of ourselves, it would not be easy to heal, rise nor soar. This self-judgment would just add inner stress and pain that will delay our healing, let alone rising or soaring. Judgment of our selves and others is dead weight on our souls. Loss and trauma are also already heavy on our spirits and adding judgmental thoughts just keep us down even more.

Many times, when we judge others, we actually project our judgment on our selves. As we let go of our judgments, we lighten up more enough to soar beyond our trials and tribulations. When we let go of our judgments, we become more re-connected to our natural core spirits which have been shaken down by our losses and tragedies.

Embracing diversity, enjoying the differences among people and marveling in the similarities of all people can help counter our tendency to be judgmental of others. By embracing diversity, we learn so much more; we learn to see the various ways that people see situations. We become more understanding of people's differences. We become more tolerant of those who seem to look different from us. Going beyond just our point of view can help us tremendously in our healing. For instance, some people, because they are used to a certain way of healing, have no tolerance for the "four-directions" type of healing. People from different cultures have different ways of helping people heal. Some people just believe in traditional medicine or some people just believe in Western medicine. However, imagine if people are open-minded to all types of healing from all over the world? This most especially applies to those who have chronic and terminal ailments.

Most traditional healing is effective when it comes to prevention of illnesses. Our Western medicine is more utilized and adhered to when it comes to acute problems. Tribal healing and spirituality have been known to help those who believe in their medicine man. A combination of both treatments and healing can certainly hopefully help when all else fails.

Opening up to colors also has to do with acceptance of people's creed, sexual orientation and socio-economic status.

It is healing to accept others as well as ourselves. We are who we are. We have a choice of accepting that or not. In reality, non-acceptance creates more internal strain within us and that could be a deterrent to soaring beyond our trauma.

Gentle Reflective Questions

1. Who did you know adhered to various types of healing for their illnesses?
2. What kind of treatment and healing do you believe in?
3. Where did you feel that you felt respected in terms of your race, creed, culture, sexual orientation, and socio-economic status?
4. Why do you think that tolerance and diversity is important?
5. When was the last time you remembered being tolerant? Intolerant?

Answers and sacred thoughts

Phoenix Miracle Pearls

"I have thought it thoroughly over; State of hermit, state of lover; we must have society; we can not spare variety."

~ Ralph Waldo Emerson

"It is never too late to give up your prejudices."

~ Henry David Thoreau

"The wise man belongs to all countries, for the home of a great soul is the whole world."

~ Democritus

Gentle Exercises for the Spirit

1. Let us take a little time to study our circle of friends. Do we have a rainbow of colors among our friends?
2. Let us think about what attracted us to our various friends.
3. Are we in touch with our unconscious biases - beliefs that have been passed on down to us by our families as we were growing up?
4. Let us think about the times when we got ill and what were our biases about the various treatments and healing?
5. Let us think about the importance of diversity and tolerance at home and in our workplace.

7. Put a loving circle around your point of view and that of others

In several organizations where I worked, my colleagues and staff know that when there are various ideas and thoughts in administrative meetings, I eventually would say "Okay, now put a circle around all your ideas and let's see what happens". As Medical Director, part of my job was to serve as a leadership voice to translate to administration the needs of the providers to make sure that their patients' clinical care was seen as priority.

Our medical meetings consist of doctors, nurse practitioners and nurses who are all bright in their own right and are opinion leaders in healthcare. This comes like a double edge sword at times. When you are leading a team with brilliant people who want their opinions heard, many times, there would be very controversial discussions because of their differences in opinions on the care of our patients. There are times when someone can get very dogmatic about their opinions with no room for flexing their thoughts and ideas. One thing, I learned quickly is that intelligent people would rather have their opinion be implemented than have administrative leaders decide for them about clinical issues. So when the discussions get way too heated and seemingly never-ending, I just tell them "to find a way to put a circle around all their ideas to come to consensus". I would tell them that I planned to go to the restroom and that when I came back, I would like one of them to speak about the consensus that they came up with. More often than not, this has actually worked very well in the teams who I worked with. These are very bright people who think very quickly and it has been amazing to see them come to a general consensus by the time I got back from the rest room.

Our late CEO, Dr. Howard Bracco was truly a master in redirecting us back to our mission after heated debates regarding patient care. He had a team of leaders who were activists in their own right and many had spearheaded creative programs that served the needs of our patients. Whenever there were heated discussions among the leadership team, he rounded up their ideas by redirecting us all back to our organization's mission and vision. That usually ended the arguments.

It is imperative for us to be able to create consensus or relax power struggles with others. We can do this by valuing other people's ideas no matter how polar opposite they are from ours. This does not mean we flex our principles. There is a balance in being able to come to a consensus without compromising our ethics and principles. These concepts can be applied to family and friendship relationships as well, and most of all to our healing, rising and soaring from our tragedies. When we lock heads with others and be able to come to a consensus about issues, we feel less stress overall. This can only help with us soaring from our losses and tragedies.

Gentle Reflective Questions

1. Who are the people who have valued your opinions?
2. When did you feel your opinions were valued at home and at work?
3. Where do you tend to get into power struggles with others?
4. Why do you think coming to a consensus and relaxing power struggles are important for healing?
5. What opinion did you have that you felt most valued about?

Answers and sacred thoughts

Phoenix Miracle Pearls

"But in every matter the consensus of opinion among all nations is to be regarded as the law of nature."

~ Cicero

"Be kind, for everyone you meet is fighting a harder battle."

~ Plato

Gentle Exercises for the Spirit

1. Let us remember a conflict at home or at work, and how you and others came to a consensus. Let us remember how we felt as we ended up in consensus.

2. Let us now think about a time when we power-struggled with someone. Let us think about what the power-struggle was about.
Remember how we relaxed the power-struggled and how we felt.

3. Let us think about a time when we felt in synch with a group of people - at home, at work, in gatherings. Let us think of the times when we were able to value the different opinions of others.

8. Believe in your life purpose

It is always beneficial for our well-being to have a life purpose. This purpose holds us and anchors us to our lives. To believe in our life purpose is to go beyond ourselves for a greater good.

Joseph Robinette Biden Jr. (Joe Biden) openly talked about how what got him through his losses and pain was "purpose". He has been able to use his painful experiences (he lost his first wife, his daughter and then his son) to help heal others through his empathy and compassion for the people who struggle.

After our family had gone through losses and tragedies, my sublimated energies went towards global medical mission and short term disaster relief work. There was something innately healing about going beyond ourselves. When we get in touch with being true vessels for a greater good, we seem to be able to withstand whatever it is to be able to serve our purpose. I know this to be true from all the global short term disaster relief work that I have done.

Believe that it was not an accident that you were born in this world.

We were all meant to be. I am currently in the midst of co-authoring a book with Dr Ashis Brahma called BE where we address the issue of Be-ing.

In his book, *The Courage to Be*, Paul Tillich insightfully alluded that "to be" is the courage to accept one's self as accepted and affirm one's self in spite of being unacceptable. Be-ing also entails our relationship with ourselves and our relationship with our Highest Source. By virtue of being human, at times the acceptance of ourselves and others may prove to be difficult. However, when we focus beyond ourselves for a greater good and when we follow our life purpose, acceptance of self and others seem more accessible to our healing souls.

When we firmly believe in our life purpose, and choose to believe that our lives have a reason more than we may ever be able to understand, something magical happens within us. We start discovering more synchronicity in our every day lives. We begin to realize that perhaps there really are no accidents in our universe. We learn to accept that we are on this earth for a reason even beyond our own. Our life purpose becomes our road map to our higher selves.

Believing in our life purpose gets us back on track in our life journey. During disasters, losses and tragedies, we tend to veer off our life map to adapt to the difficult situations. Our belief in our life purpose can serve as an emotional and spiritual anchor in our healing and allows us to soar above life's challenges.

Gentle Reflective Questions

1. Who has been helpful in guiding you towards your life purpose?
2. When did you get in touch with your life purpose?
3. What is your life purpose?
4. Where do you think will catapult you towards your life purpose?
5. Why do you feel that a life purpose is important to our healing and soaring from our experiences?

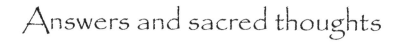

Answers and sacred thoughts

Phoenix Miracle Pearls

"The purpose of life is not to be happy. It is to be useful, to be honorable, to be compassionate, to have it make some difference that you have lived and have lived well".

~ Ralph Waldo Emerson

"The mystery of human existence lies not in just staying alive, but in finding something to live for".

~ Fyodor Dostoyevsky

Gentle Exercises for the Spirit

1. Let us visualize what would make our spirits soar. Let us envision ourselves in the midst of our life purpose. Let us contemplate about where our skill sets can be used the most. Let us think about where we can go beyond ourselves and contribute to our greater good.
2. Let us think about our life purpose. We can ask ourselves whether we are in the midst of our life purpose or have we gone off the path?
3. Let us also think about a life purpose that is dynamic and all-evolving. Or it could be something simple and true. Let us remember that as we grow, our experiences make us more in tune with the purpose of our lives.

9. Imagine Peace. Imagine Hope. Imagine love.

Our imaginations are limitless. Our minds can bask in the glory of being able to imagine just about anything. If so, why not imagine peace, hope and love. This is the subtitle of my coffee table book entitled "Your Compassionate Nature". If we put our minds to it, and focus, we can achieve the state that gives us peace, which then gives us hope which then makes it easier for us to love.

Visualizations and imaginations are powerful in and of themselves. When we visualize, we are also able to manifest our visualizations. The results of these manifestations lead us to create many incredible things that serve the good of our world. Leonardo da Vinci visualized and imagined ideas that he manifested into profound art works, sketches and drawings that led to the invention of many things that now help mankind.

Just imagine if a critical mass of people start imagining Peace, Hope and Love altogether. Some people believe for instance that if people meditate more about peace, hope and love, the profound energies of meditation can positively affect people in our communities. Prayers and meditations help us focus on these visualizations and manifestations.

When we have more peace, hope and love in our hearts, this can add to our going beyond our tragedies and losses. The lesser the stressors and conflicts and chaos within, the more balanced we feel. The quality and positivity of our attitudes and minds help in our healing from various circumstances. If we can overthink ourselves to the point were we become ill, imagine thinking so positively that we start feeling better. When our minds feel better, our bodies hopefully start to feel better and vice-versa.

Gentle Reflective Questions

1. Who do you know are peaceful, hopeful and loving persons?
2. What do you think helped them to be peaceful, hopeful and loving?
3. Where do you feel peaceful, hopeful and loving?
4. When did you ever feel peaceful, hopeful and loving?
5. Why do you think is it important to be imagine peace, imagine, hope and imagine love? How does this help with our healing, rising and soaring?

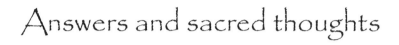

Answers and sacred thoughts

Phoenix Miracle Pearls

"Peace comes from within. Do not seek it without"

~ Gautama Buddha

"However long the night, the dawn will break."

~ African proverb (Hausa tribe)

"Hope springs eternal".

~ Alexander Pope

Gentle Exercises for the Spirit

1. Let us close our eyes and remember a time when we felt much Peace.
2. Let us remember a time when we felt much Hope.
3. Let us remember a time when we loved and felt love back as well.
4. Let us remember when we felt Peace, Hope and Love all at the same time.
5. Let us feel Peace, Hope and Love filling our hearts at present.

10. Love with all your heart

It is a profound soulful decision to love with all our heart. William Shakespeare wrote about the path of true love not being easy. Khalil Gibran wrote about love: "To know the pain of too much tenderness, to be wounded by your own understanding of love, and to bleed willingly and joyfully, to wake up at dawn with a winged heart, and give thanks for another day of loving". Rumi mused about the heart having to be broken many times before it opens.

Love comes in many forms and many times it comes to us suddenly. God has a way of directing the course of love even when we think that loving is through our own volition.

When I first met Lawrence, he and I and his family, knew it was love at first sight. At that time, I was just quite happy traveling the world volunteering and doing my short term global missions and I did this for many years. I had been single for a long time since my previous divorce.

At that time I was dealing with losses and a family tragedy that eventually gave me the courage to serve others who suffered disasters, losses and tragedies around the world. When I met Lawrence, it was as if the universe conspired for me to be with him. And there was no turning back. That was the way it felt. I initially had my own resistances because I did not want my heart to be broken nor did I want to break anybody's heart. Yet what I felt for him was beyond compelling, almost overwhelming.

It also happened when it was so least expected. I met Lawrence at a time when I was doing short term volunteer mission work at the Pine Ridge reservation. His sister Rosalie was a grassroots worker and she was my main contact during my short stay there to in some way help there, no matter how small the help, during their back to back snow blizzards.

Loving with all my heart became a collaborative decision between God and me. What deeply attracted me to Lawrence was his profound sense of spirituality. He was a sun-dancer for many years and spent his life at that time walking in prayer while preparing to sun-dance in the summers. As a Lakota warrior he chose to sacrifice by sun-dancing whereby the sun-dancers fasted for four days without food nor water and they prayerfully danced from sun up to sun down. The spiritual concept behind sun-dancing is "so that the people may live". There was a time when the Lakotas and other Native Americans had to hide their ceremonies and rituals because they were not allowed by the colonizers to practice their spirituality freely. I eventually learned a lot of the Lakota way from Lawrence, his family and the community I served.

To love with all my heart means to be openly vulnerable and that can be truly anxiety-provoking. It means surrendering to our Creator our love for another person. For in reality, this commitment of loving with all our hearts is a vow between God and ourselves.

Loving someone gives us much courage. Opening up our vulnerabilities to someone is all about choosing to trust. When we love someone deeply, we harvest a lot of positive energies within us that can only help in our healing and soaring above the tragedies we may experience.

Gentle Reflective Questions

1. Who have you loved with all your heart and who do you feel has loved you with all their hearts?
2. When did you feel the most loved? When did you feel you gave the most love?
3. What makes you feel loved?
4. Where did you feel the most love?
5. Why do you feel that loving with all your heart is important in our healing and soaring from our tribulations?

Answers and sacred thoughts

Phoenix Miracle Pearls

"To love or have loved, that is enough. Ask nothing further. There is no other pearl to be found in the dark folds of life."

~ Victor Hugo

"We loved with a love that was more than love".

~ Edgar Allan Poe

"Love is the bridge between you and everything".

~ Rumi

Gentle Exercises for the Spirit

1. Let us contemplate about Love. Love in all its forms. Love for a significant person. Love for family. Love for friends.
   Love for our world. Love for self. Love for our Creator.
2. Let us ponder about what Love means to us.
3. Let us contemplate on how we have loved others. Let us remember how others have loved us.
4. Let us keep in mind the power of Love and how it can heal us. Let us remember those times when we were able to soar beyond our tragedies and losses because of Love.

11. Volunteer. Volunteer. Volunteer.

Once you volunteer, your spirit naturally soars. You will love the feeling and, even through difficult moments that may arise in your life, you want to experience it again and again. To volunteer takes you instantly beyond yourself. It guides you to reach into your spiritual resources, and to discover that they are still plentiful. To volunteer is to give your best compassion and kindness to others.

Many of us who have experienced heartbreaks, tragedies, losses and disasters eventually realize that we have in some general way evolved into more understanding and empathetic people. We have walked other peoples' moccasins through life lessons derived from our own experiences. As volunteers, we are able to reach out and console those who are suffering just the way we were at one time. Because we understand their feelings and their plight to some degree, we experience their human presence more deeply. This helps us realize something really magnificent about life, something which is bigger even than the tragedy and dislocation of the present moment. We are all interconnected through love, and will remain so throughout eternity. Volunteering helps us experience this as a living reality, not merely a beautiful concept.

After a family tragedy, it was compelling for me to volunteer in Thailand after the tsunami. Who else would understand the meaning of disaster and suffering but one who has also gone through a tragedy? Instinctively, I sorted through my skill-sets, searching for what was best in me, in order to effectively serve others. Reaching out to the people who were suffering seemed the most natural thing to do. By striving to give my best, I was able to give many beleaguered people hope that they would not only survive the tragic situation, but that they too could eventually soar like the phoenix from their ashes of despair.

My brother Jun, later asked me if I could write something for his web site about the reasons why people volunteer. He was a first-responder and an all-around hero for all of us in the family. This was adapted from what I wrote for him:

Why do we volunteer?

There comes a time in our lives when we become cognizant of the gratitude we feel for everything we are and have become. And we realize the meaning of an old saying, "From those whom much is given, much is expected."

Even though many have suffered disasters, losses and tragedies, there are those – the ones I call Phoenix Miracle people – who rise from their ashes of devastation and give hope and light to others. These are the extraordinary people who face their spiritual challenges to find richer meaning and new discernment in what they have learned from the uncontrollable trials and tribulations of life that at one time rendered them powerless. They heal, they stand, then soar and take action to spread "the wisdom to know the difference." They shine their lights on other souls who may be in need.

People volunteer for reasons beyond the tragedies and losses they have gone through. Many volunteer because they simply have it in their loving hearts to serve others. Most of us grew up being taught spiritual tenets upholding love of God and others as the principal mandates of goodness. Volunteerism is a noble avenue to give one's self. And to give of our selves is the height of what love is about. Even if in other ways we may fall short of absolute goodness by virtue of being human beings. To volunteer is to be connected with people in our profundity. And it is through this connection that we learn to appreciate the significance of our very existence. To volunteer is to "till our souls," to move our spirits, to offer our selves, to be launched toward our higher purpose.

To volunteer: to serve, to care, to love.

To volunteer: love in action.

Gentle Reflective Questions

1. What skills and talents do you possess?
2. When did you feel compelled to volunteer to help in a situation?
3. Why did you decide to volunteer? How did you feel when you volunteered?
4. Who supported you in you in your desire to volunteer?
5. Where did you volunteer?

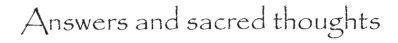

Answers and sacred thoughts

Phoenix Miracle Pearls

"If I can stop one heart from breaking, I shall not live in vain. If I can ease one life the aching, or cool one pain; or help a fainting robin unto his nest again, I shall not live in vain."

~ Emily Dickinson

"The best way to find yourself is to lose yourself in the service of others

~ Gautama Buddha

"The meaning of life is to find your gift. The purpose of life is to give it away".

~ William Shakespeare

Gentle Exercises of the Spirit

1. Gentle thoughts:
   "I have it in me to volunteer."
   "I have skills and talents to offer others."
   "I have many gifts to offer our world".
2. Gentle words: Take three slow breaths, breathing in through your nose then out through your mouth. Whisper to yourself our gentle thoughts.
3. Gentle actions: Find a cause. Ask yourself what you are best at and then share it with others. Look for volunteer work in local, national, or international service organizations. It is quite easy to just go online and Google the phrase Network for Good. You will be able to pick a non-profit organization whose mission inspires you, and that may have volunteer work that is compatible with your skills. Ask your church. Ask your area schools, or your children's schools, what you can do to be of service. Volunteer to help in a nursing home or an orphanage. Volunteer to uplift a cause. There are many ways to volunteer. Pick a cause which you feel can use the things you know and can do.

Volunteer. Volunteer. Volunteer.

12. Visualize yourself as the Phoenix

- A Phoenix Miracle~

The phoenix is a phenomenal symbol of life, vitality, resurrection and which then gives way to soaring to give compassion, love and light to our world. As human beings we have all experienced losses, tragedies and disasters. The phoenix miracle is the ability of each one of us to rise from the ashes of despair and help others with what we have already experienced.

My sister Marissa did the painting of the cover of this book. The phoenix in the painting is looking towards the sun. When my sister and I would dialogue about anything, I would come up with an idea and she brilliantly manifested it through her art. She was a consummate artist through and through and never seemed to have any artist's blocks. My sister was filled with creative energy and she used her artistic abilities to help people as she was an Expressive Therapist. She is now one of our angels in heaven. She was my very best friend.

There comes a time when we have an inner knowing that we are back to our stable core, even stronger than before. We are also now way past survival mode. We are able to look back and be able to learn from the circumstances that hurt us. Every now and then we may still feel a twinge of pain yet you now understand more that some of that pain has been part of your growth and healing. You may even feel different now because you have evolved. You have gone beyond what you may have even imagined.

Obviously, there will be times that may cause us to take a back step for whatever reason. To soar is not a straight line. We are human after all. Just know that all that is alright. Just keep on looking towards the light. Stay steady and never give up. You are much stronger than you have ever been because you have been tested by the fire of life. You will know your courage and strength each day until you eventually emanate your light within to serve others.

You are now ready to soar and give compassion, light and love to the world. Your life experiences and circumstances will serve to help and even heal others by being an exemplar of hope, courage and love.

Soar, fly high, and shine your light out there!

Soar and be the Phoenix Miracle that you are!

~The beginning~

Made in the USA
Las Vegas, NV
01 February 2021